P9-CQV-064

It's My State!

OREGON
The Beaver State

Ruth Bjorklund, Joyce Hart, and Jacqueline Laks Gorman

Cavendish
Square

New York

Published in 2016 by Cavendish Square Publishing, LLC
243 5th Avenue, Suite 136, New York, NY 10016

Third Edition

Website: cavendishsq.com

This publication represents the opinions and views of the author based on his or her personal experience, knowledge, and research. The information in this book serves as a general guide only. The author and publisher have used their best efforts in preparing this book and disclaim liability rising directly or indirectly from the use and application of this book.

CPSIA Compliance Information: Batch #WS15CSQ

All websites were available and accurate when this book was sent to press.

Library of Congress Cataloging-in-Publication Data

Bjorklund, Ruth.
Oregon / Ruth Bjorklund, Joyce Hart, Jacqueline Laks Gorman.
pages cm. — (It's my state!)
Includes bibliographical references and index.
ISBN 978-1-62713-172-8 (hardcover) ISBN 978-1-62713-174-2 (ebook)
1. Oregon—Juvenile literature. I. Hart, Joyce, 1954- II. Gorman, Jacqueline Laks, 1955- III. Title.

F876.3.B55 2016
979.5—dc23

2014049214

Editorial Director: David McNamara
Editor: Fletcher Doyle
Copy Editor: Rebecca Rohan
Art Director: Jeffrey Talbot
Designer: Joseph Macri
Senior Production Manager: Jennifer Ryder-Talbot
Production Editor: Renni Johnson
Photo Research: J8 Media

The photographs, maps, and illustrations in this book are used by permission and through the courtesy of: Josemaria Toscano/Shutterstock.com, cover; Peter Arnold, Inc./Alamy, 4; Candus Camera/Shutterstock.com, 4; D. Hurst/Alamy, 4; Leroy Simon/Visuals Unlimited/Getty Images, 5; Bruce Coleman Inc./Alamy, 5; Peter Lilja/Getty Images, 5; Peter Kim/Shutterstock.com, 6; Marc Muench/Getty Images, 8; George Ostertag/Superstock, 9; Westgraphix LLC, 10; Stock Connection/Superstock, 11; Terry Donnelly/Getty Images, 13; Randy Wells/Getty Images, 14; Danita Delimont/Gallo Images/Getty Images, 14; Orygun/File: Mouth of Lava River Cave.jpg/Wikimedia Commons, 14; Panoramic Images/Getty Images, 15; Pfly from Pugetopolis/File: Aquarium Tunnel. jpg/Wikimedia Commons, 15; Finetooth/File: Wallowa Lake Tramway.jpg/Wikimedia Commons, 15; Jonathan Kingston/Getty Images, 17; Greg Vaughn/Alamy, 18; Jim and Jamie Dutcher/Getty Images, 19; Mark Conlin/Alamy, 20; Jeff Rotman/Getty Images, 20; William Leaman/Alamy, 20; Corbis RF/Alamy, 21; Raciro/iStock Photo, 21; Shanna Baker/Getty Images, 21; MPI/Getty Images, 22; North Wind Picture Archives/Alamy, 24; Oregon Historical Society OrHi93065, 25; Richard H. and Adeline J. Fleischaker Collection, 1996/Bridgeman Art Library, 26; Greg Vaughn/Alamy, 29; Denis Frates/Alamy, 32; Time & Life Pictures/Getty Images, 33; Steve Satushek/Getty Images, 34; Ilene MacDonald/Alamy, 34; Amoore5000/File: Farewell Bend Park, Bend, Oregon.jpg/Wikimedia Commons, 35; Serenethos/Shutterstock.com, 35; Fotosearch/Getty Images, 36; North Wind Picture Archives/Alamy, 38; Gerry Ellis/Getty Images, 39; Danita Delimont/Alamy, 41; Brian Stevenson/Aurora/Getty Images, 44; Buyenlarge/Getty Images, 47; Frazer Harrison/Getty Images for Coachella, 48; Frazer Harrison/Getty Images, 48; WireImage/Getty Images, 48; Frank Micelotta/Getty Images, 49; Joe McNally/Getty Images, 49; Rob Kim/Getty Images, 49; North Wind Picture Archives, 50; Public Domain/File: McCants Stewart 1910.png/Wikimedia Commons, 51; D. Hurst/Alamy, 53; Bates Littlehales/National Geographic/Getty Images, 54; George Ostertag/Age Fotostock/Superstock, 54; Jamie Hooper/Shutterstock.com, 55; William Mancebo/Getty Images, 55; JPL Designs/Shutterstock.com, 56; Ilene MacDonald/Alamy, 58; FogStock/Alamy, 59; Andre Jenny/Alamy, 60; Joyce Naltchayan/AFP/Getty Images, 62; Bill Peters/The Denver Post/Getty Images, 62; Amber Lynn Lane/File: Governor Barbara Roberts.jpg/Wikimedia Commons, 62; Ravitej Khalsa, 63; MacDuff Everton/National Geographic/Getty Images, 64; National Geographic/Getty Images, 66; Bruce Forster/Getty Images, 67; AGStockUSA/Alamy, 68; George Ostertag/Superstock, 68; Cavan Images/Getty Images, 69; Scott Markewitz/Getty Images, 69; Eleana/Shutterstock.com, 70; Age Fotostock/Superstock, 72; Christopher Santoro, 74; Sherri R. Camp/Shutterstock.com, 75; American Spirit/Shutterstock.com, 75; Christopher Santoro, 76.

Printed in the United States of America

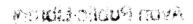

OREGON
CONTENTS

A Quick Look at Oregon 4

1. The Beaver State 7
Oregon County Map 10
Oregon Population by County 11
10 Key Sites 14
10 Key Plants and Animals 20

2. From the Beginning 23
The Native People 26
Making an Oregon Trail Covered Wagon 30
10 Key Cities 34
10 Key Dates 43

3. The People 45
10 Key People 48
10 Key Events 54

4. How the Government Works 57
Political Figures from Oregon 62
You Can Make a Difference 63

5. Making a Living 65
10 Key Industries 68
Recipe for Cheddar Cheese Crackers 70

Oregon State Map 74
Oregon Map Skills 75
State Flag, Seal, and Song 76
Glossary 77
More About Oregon 78
Index 79

A QUICK LOOK AT

State Tree: Douglas Fir

The largest Douglas fir measures more than three hundred feet. Eight out of ten evergreens in Western Oregon are Douglas firs. Named after a Scottish botanist, the Douglas fir was recognized as the state tree in 1936.

State Fruit: Pear

The first pear tree seedlings were brought to Oregon in 1847. Pear trees thrive in Oregon's temperate climate and farmers produce more than eight hundred million pears each year. Varieties include Bosc, Bartlett, and Anjou. The pear became the state fruit in 2005.

State Flower: Oregon Grape

The Oregon grape plant is an evergreen bush that produces small, bell-shaped, yellow flowers in the spring and blue berries in the fall. The berries are edible when ripe. The Oregon grape, named the state flower in 1899, is common along the coast.

OREGON

★ State Insect: Oregon Swallowtail Butterfly

This black-and-yellow butterfly is native to the Northwest. It prefers the dry, Eastern part of the state where it lives in sagebrush, especially along the Columbia, Snake, and Deschutes Rivers. It was named the state insect in 1979.

★ State Bird: Western Meadowlark

The western meadowlark is a sweet-sounding songbird found in native grass prairies in Eastern Oregon that migrates west in winter. It uses its long, sharp beak to peck out grubs and seeds in the soil. In 1927, school children voted to make the western meadowlark the state bird.

★ State Animal: Beaver

The beaver was almost completely wiped out by fur trappers. Today, the beaver is protected by state law, and can again be found along many of Oregon's rivers. They are called nature's engineers because of their ability to build complex dams. The beaver is Oregon State University's mascot.

The rocky coast is one of the many different features of the geography of Oregon.

The Beaver State

Oregon is the southern-most state in the region known as the Pacific Northwest. It features a wide diversity of nature—mossy rainforests, snow-covered volcanic mountains, lush river valleys, and hot, dry deserts. Oregon seems more like several different states, rather than just one.

Oregonians are proud of their state's natural beauty. The Cascade mountain range divides the state into east and west sections, creating differences in climate, natural habitats, and lifestyles. From bighorn sheep to wild salmon, raging rivers to desert plains, wheat fields to orchards, Oregonians on both sides of the Cascades enjoy a unique environment and way of life.

A Land of Contrasts

Oregon is the ninth largest state in the nation with a land area of 95,997 square miles (248,631 square kilometers). The state is rectangular. From east to west, it is about 400 miles (650 kilometers) wide, and from north to south, it is around 250 miles (400 km) long. Idaho lies along Oregon's eastern border, separated by the Snake River in the north and the Owyhee Mountains in the south. Oregon's entire western border faces the Pacific Ocean. Washington State lies to the north separated by the Blue Mountains and the Columbia River. Oregon shares its southern border with Nevada and California.

Mount Hood, in the Cascade Mountains, is the highest point in the state at 11,250 feet (3,429 m).

The Cascade Range and the Coast Range are Oregon's major mountain ranges, formed more than two hundred million years ago when the North American continent and the floor of the Pacific Ocean shifted. Earth's surface layer is made up of thick sections of rock called plates. These plates move very slowly. On Oregon's western shore, the ocean plate bumped into the land plate and slid underneath. The ocean plate pushed the land upward, creating the Coast Range. The ocean plate continued to move, heating up the rock and melting it. The hot liquid rock eventually gushed to the surface in the form of **lava**. After many lava explosions, a line of volcanoes formed, creating the Cascade Range.

Weather has created many of Oregon's physical features. Rainclouds frequently blow in from the ocean and become trapped by the mountains, causing precipitation to fall on the mountains' western slopes. The Cascades are colder and higher in elevation than the Coast Range. Winter precipitation there often comes in the form of heavy, wet snow. Water flowing down the mountainsides has created numerous lakes and rivers. But once clouds pass over the Cascades to the eastern side, the moisture in the air has drained. That is why it rains and snows less often in eastern Oregon, and why eastern Oregon has dry, desert-like conditions.

The Western Coast

Oregon has one of the most scenic coastlines in the world. In some places, sheer cliffs of the Coast Range rise straight out of the sea. Elsewhere are sandy beaches and large rock formations called "sea stacks." More than twenty rivers flow out of the Coast Range into the ocean, creating bodies of water called **estuaries**. The mixture of salt and fresh water in estuaries spurs the growth of a variety of plants and animals. Oregon's coastal forests belong to the only temperate rainforest in North America. In the center of the coast is the Oregon Dunes area, the largest expanse of coastal sand dunes in the country.

Oregon Borders	
North:	Washington
South:	California Nevada
East:	Idaho
West:	Pacific Ocean

The Willamette Valley

The Willamette Valley lies east of the Coast Range and west of the Cascade Mountains. At the northern end of the valley is Portland, the state's largest city. Near the southern end of the valley is Eugene, the second largest city. Other cities include Corvallis and Salem, the state capital.

The Willamette River runs through the fertile Willamette Valley.

OREGON

County	Population	County	Population	County	Population
Baker County	16,018	Hood River County	22,675	Polk County	76,794
Benton County	86,591	Jackson County	208,545	Sherman County	1,731
Clackamas County	388,263	Jefferson County	21,145	Tillamook County	25,317
Clatsop County	37,244	Josephine County	83,306	Umatilla County	76,720
Columbia County	49,344	Klamath County	65,910	Union County	25,652
Coos County	62,282	Lake County	7,820	Wallowa County	6,814
Crook County	20,815	Lane County	356,212	Wasco County	25,477
Curry County	22,339	Lincoln County	46,350	Washington County	554,996
Deschutes County	165,954	Linn County	118,765	Wheeler County	1,381
Douglas County	106,940	Malheur County	30,479	Yamhill County	100,725
Gilliam County	1,947	Marion County	323,614		
Grant County	7,283	Morrow County	11,336		
Harney County	7,146	Multnomah County	766,135		

Source: US Bureau of the Census, 2010

The quality of Tillamook Cheese is monitored by an association started in 1909 in Tillamook County.

When pioneers crossed the Cascade Mountains and entered the Willamette Valley, many thought they had reached a garden paradise. The valley proved to be an ideal place to settle, with rich soil, plentiful forests, and many fruit-bearing bushes. The weather was mild, the land was flat and easy to farm, and rain fell in abundance. Today, farms line the valley, and the area is home to more than two million people.

The Cascade Mountains

Oregon's highest elevations are in the Cascade Mountains. The state's highest point is the cone-shaped summit of Mount Hood, east of Portland. Mount Hood is 11,239 feet (3,426 meters) high. Other major peaks include Mounts Jefferson, Washington, and Bachelor, and the triple peaks of the Three Sisters. These volcanic mountains are snow-capped by **glaciers** year round. The Cascades stretch from Northern California to British Columbia, Canada, and while there are some active volcanoes, few have erupted in Oregon, the last occurring on Mount Hood more than two hundred years ago.

Crater Lake, located in Oregon's Southern Cascades, was created when an ancient volcano, called Mount Mazama, exploded and then collapsed into an enormous hole. The hole filled with water. The lake is almost 2,000 feet (600 m) deep. It is the deepest lake in the United States and the seventh-deepest lake in the world.

The Central Cascades region is a high plateau containing stately ponderosa pines and alpine lakes. The Central Cascades receive more rain than eastern Oregon but more sun than western Oregon and is home to the fast-growing cities of Bend and Redmond. Further south is the city of Ashland, which is famous for its yearly Shakespeare festival.

The Eastern High Desert

More than half of Oregon lies on the eastern side of the Cascades. The Snake River runs through Hells Canyon, which is the deepest river **gorge** in the United States, deeper even than the Grand Canyon. From the highest point on the eastern rim, the canyon is about 8,000 feet (2,400 m) deep. East of Hells Canyon, near the Wallowa Mountains and the Blue Mountains, are large ranches and farms. The city of Pendleton, known for its annual rodeo, is the area's commercial center.

A Place to Park

Oregon has twelve national forests, one national park, two national historical parks, and four national monuments. The state also has two national recreation areas, 2.5 million acres [1,011,714 hectares] of protected wilderness, and seventeen national wildlife refuges.

Hells Canyon is the deepest river gorge in the United States.

South of Pendleton, there are fewer towns, but wide expanses of wheat fields, ranches, and sagebrush-covered hills. In the southeast is the Hart Mountain National Antelope Refuge, which protects three hundred species of wildlife, including pronghorn antelope, mule deer, and bighorn sheep. Other towns, such as John Day and Baker City, were established by gold miners during the gold rush of the 1860s. In the rugged landscape near John Day are the John Day **Fossil** Beds, which contain forty thousand plant and animal fossils, including the cousins of elephants, camels, rhinoceroses, and saber-toothed tigers that once roamed eastern Oregon.

The Climate

There are few other states that have temperature differences like Oregon's. The average high temperature along the coast in July is only 65 degrees Fahrenheit (18 degrees Celsius) while the average high in eastern Oregon is 86°F (31°C). The average low temperature in January is 40°F (4°C) on the coast and 22°F (−6°C) in eastern Oregon.

People on the coast experience cool summers and mild winters. Fog often hugs the coast and the Coast Range receives a great deal of rain. Willamette Valley summers are usually warm and dry, but from fall to spring, a steady supply of rain falls. Only an

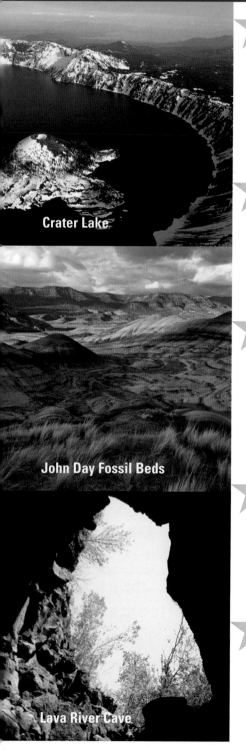

Crater Lake

John Day Fossil Beds

Lava River Cave

1. Columbia River Gorge

The Columbia River Gorge was formed fifteen thousand years ago, at the end of the last ice age, when warming weather melted massive ice fields. This flooded the gorge. The floodwaters carved huge cliffs and created numerous waterfalls.

2. Crater Lake National Park

The 20-square-mile (53 sq km) Crater Lake was created six thousand years ago when a volcano collapsed suddenly. Although the lake is surrounded by deep snow in winter, the lake rarely freezes because there are hot springs underground.

3. Hart Mountain National Antelope Refuge

This 278,000-acre (112,503 ha) wildlife refuge is located above the remote Warner Valley. Dedicated in 1936, Hart Mountain protects more than three hundred species of wildlife. Hikers will find views of the valley, natural hot springs, and ancient Native American petroglyphs.

4. John Day Fossil Beds

Fifty million years ago, the dry, rugged landscape near John Day was covered by a prehistoric ocean and tropical forests. Today, visitors can hike its 14,000 acres (5,666 ha) and see fossil beds containing the remains of plant and animal life.

5. Lava River Cave

This ancient lava tube near Bend is part of the Newberry Crater National Monument. Lava tubes are created by hot flowing lava that solidifies above ground to form a tunnel. Hikers must descend 150 stairs to reach the mile-long (1.6 km) tube.

6. Mount Hood

The towering, cone-shaped peak of Mount Hood is a major feature of the Pacific Crest Trail. It is a wilderness destination for hikers, fishers, campers, and skiers. There are twelve glaciers on Mount Hood. Skiers and snowboarders enjoy its trails year round.

7. Oregon Coast Aquarium

One popular exhibit at the Oregon Coast Aquarium in Newport is called Deep Passage. Visitors walk through a pathway of clear tubes deep underwater to be surrounded by rays, fish, crabs, and sharks.

8. Oregon Dunes National Recreation Area

The Oregon Dunes extend for 40 miles (64 km) along the coast near Florence. Some dunes are more than 500 feet (152 m) tall. First-time visitors should hike with a guide; it is easy to become lost amid the enormous mounds of sand.

9. Rogue River

Below Crater Lake, underground springs burst out and shoot past lava fields deposited by Mount Mazama, creating the wild and scenic Rogue River. The river is clear, cold, and fast-moving as it takes its 250-mile (402 km) westward course to the southern Oregon coast.

10. Wallowa Lake Tramway

At Wallowa Lake, in Joseph, a tramway runs to the summit of an 8,150-foot (2,484 m) mountain. Visible from there are the Wallowa Mountains, Chief Joseph's former hunting grounds, Washington and Idaho, and the Snake River.

Mount Hood

Oregon Coast Aquarium

Wallowa Lake Tramway

occasional snowstorm passes over the valley and the snow rarely remains on the ground more than a few days.

The Cascade Mountains receive the most snow, and skiing is a popular sport. Many of the tallest mountains in the Cascades receive hundreds of inches of snow each year. Crater Lake National Park once received a snowfall of 879 inches.

The people who live in eastern Oregon experience extreme temperatures. The lowest temperature ever recorded in eastern Oregon was in Seneca in 1933, when the temperature dropped to −54°F (−48°C). The highest recorded temperature occurred in Pendleton in 1898, when the thermometer reached 119°F (48°C). In the Blue and Wallowa Mountains, snow can begin falling in August and not melt until May.

Rainfall and Bodies of Water

People who live outside of Oregon often believe that it rains there all the time. However, Portland receives less rainfall than New York City. In the desert areas of eastern Oregon, a mere 8 inches (20 cm) of rain is common. The Blue and Wallowa Mountains receive an average of 20 inches (50 cm) each year. The Willamette Valley receives about 35 inches (90 cm) annually while the Coast Range receives a hundred or more inches. In 1996, Laurel Mountain in the Coast Range had a record-breaking 204 inches (518 cm) of rain. The coastal city of Astoria is the third wettest city in the nation.

In Their Own Words

"We're proud to have filmed all four corners of the state. However, Oregon is the kind of place that the more you see, the more you realize you've missed and haven't seen yet!"
—Ben Canales, photographer and filmmaker

Oregon's many rivers and streams supply drinking water, electricity (through a series of hydropower dams), and recreational activities. Important rivers include the Columbia River and the Snake River. Emptying into the Columbia, the Willamette River runs north for more than 300 miles (480 km) on the west side of the Cascades and the Deschutes runs 300 miles (480 km) on the east side. Other major rivers include the John Day River in eastern Oregon, the Rogue River in the southwest, the Grande Ronde in the northeast, and the Klamath River in the southeast.

The Columbia River cuts across the Cascades through the scenic Columbia River Gorge. This canyon drops 4,000 feet (1,200 m) and is 80 miles (130 km) long. The highest waterfall in Oregon is Multnomah Falls, located east of Portland along the Columbia River Gorge. At 620 feet (190 m), Multnomah Falls is among the tallest waterfalls in the United States.

Benson Bridge crosses over Multnomah Falls.

The deep snow in the mountains feeds many lakes. Crater Lake is the deepest lake in the United States, and Wallowa Lake in eastern Oregon is famous for its clear water. Some lakes in southeastern Oregon are surprisingly salty and completely dry up in the summer months.

The Pacific Ocean, which forms Oregon's entire western boundary, is one of the state's most important bodies of water. Although the waters of the ocean are often too cold for swimming, Oregonians enjoy walking the beach and going crabbing, fishing, and clam digging.

Plants and Wildlife

Nearly half of Oregon is covered in thick forests of cedar, fir, pine, spruce, and hemlock trees, as well as red vine maples, rhododendrons, and madrones. When settlers first came to Oregon, they encountered ancient forests where trees were several hundred years old and astonishing in size. The tallest tree in Oregon today is a 750-year-old Sitka spruce, which stands 206 feet (62 m) high and is 52 feet (15 m) around. Only about 10 percent of the old forests remain today; the rest have been cut down. Some of the best places to see these old-growth forests are near Cave Junction in southern Oregon; the Oregon Caves on the coast; Union Creek, near Crater Lake; Lost Lake in Mount Hood National Forest; and

Logging has reduced the size of Oregon's beautiful old-growth forests.

the Three Sisters Wilderness area in central Oregon. In addition to trees, there are many wild edible berries, such as salmonberry, huckleberry, marionberry, and thimbleberry. Fast-growing blackberry bushes are abundant in western Oregon.

Ferns are found throughout Oregon's damp soils. Wood fern, sword fern, and maidenhair are plentiful in western forests. The horsetail fern—which is not technically a fern—springs up from the ground looking a little like asparagus, but it eventually opens its needlelike spines, giving it the appearance of a horse's tail. The damp forests also produce mosses, lichen, and mushrooms.

Forest-dwelling animals include deer, coyotes, foxes, and minks. Remote areas are home to elk, bighorn sheep, mountain goats, bobcats, cougars, and wolves. One of Oregon's best-known creatures is the banana slug. Living in the damp soils of Oregon, the slimy, yellow-green banana slug can grow more than 6 inches (15 cm) long. Slugs eat plants and flowers, which is a problem for Oregon's gardeners.

Oregon is home to more than five hundred species of birds, including songbirds, raptors, woodpeckers, and owls. Many birds pass through Oregon on their migratory journeys. There are numerous species of shorebirds, seabirds, and waterfowl including ducks, geese, egrets, herons, gulls, puffins, cormorants, and loons.

Fish have always played an important role in Oregon, not only as a major source of food, but also as a symbol of the state's bounty. There are many types of freshwater fish in Oregon, such as trout, bass, catfish, and giant sturgeon, a prehistoric fish found deep in the Columbia River. Salmon and steelhead (a large trout that lives most of its life at sea) grow to adulthood by living in the ocean and eating smaller fish. In spring and fall, salmon and steelhead return to the rivers where they were born to lay their eggs. After the salmon mate, they die, but many steelhead return to sea for a few more years. Wildlife officials enforce strict rules to help save and protect the state's wild fish. They operate fish hatcheries, and in many rivers, require sport fishers to release the fish they have caught. In the Pacific Ocean, commercial and sport fishers catch salmon, cod, halibut, and crab. The red rock crab is native to Oregon.

Endangered Animals

Throughout history, numerous animal species have become **extinct**. Sometimes it is a natural process, but more recently, animal habitats have been destroyed because of human interference. When an animal population gets dangerously low, federal or state governments may label the species "threatened" or "endangered" and enact laws to help the species survive.

Endangered animals in Oregon include the gray wolf, the Columbian white-tailed deer, the short-tailed albatross, different types of sea turtles, and the Fender's blue butterfly. Certain types of salmon are also endangered. Threatened species include the Canada lynx, the northern spotted owl, and the Oregon silverspot butterfly.

The gray wolf is endangered in Oregon.

Chinook Salmon

Giant Pacific Octopus

Great Blue Heron

1. Chinook salmon

This is the largest salmon in the Pacific Northwest. After hatching in freshwater streams, the young swim to the ocean to feed for a few years. Later, they return to their birthplace to mate and then die. On that journey, they battle currents, waterfalls, and dams.

2. Cougar

The cougar is the second largest cat in North America. It needs a large territory, such as the Blue Mountains, to hunt for deer, elk, bighorn sheep, and other mammals. There are more than five thousand cougars in Oregon, but they are shy and sightings are rare.

3. Giant Pacific Octopus

The world's largest octopus averages 16 feet (5 m) in length and 110 pounds (50 kilograms). It hides in rocks, sea grass, or reefs, and can change color. With its sharp, beaklike mouth, it eats fish, lobsters, shrimp, sharks and seabirds.

4. Great Blue Heron

In Oregon, the great blue heron is found along the Pacific shore or along the banks of some of Oregon's great rivers, such as the Rogue. The bird's feathers are a bluish-gray. Its wingspan can be as large as 6 feet (2 m).

5. Hairy Woodpecker

The medium-sized woodpecker has a striped head and a long, powerful bill. It feeds on beetles, ants, spiders, and seeds found in tree bark. After a forest fire, hairy woodpeckers gather to feed on dead trees infested with pine beetles.

6. Juniper

Juniper is a fragrant evergreen bush or tree. It tolerates heat and cold, and needs little water. The wood is used mainly as fuel or for building fences. The berries are used as a spice. Eastern Oregon has one of the largest juniper forests in the world.

7. Northern Spotted Owl

The northern spotted owl is on Oregon's threatened species list. It is also threatened in Washington and California because its habitat—old-growth forests—is quickly disappearing due to logging.

8. Oregon Iris

This tough plant with a pretty lavender flower is found throughout western Oregon. Native Americans used the plant to make rope, bags, and animal traps sturdy enough to capture elk. The Oregon iris was also ideal for making fishing nets because it floats.

9. Ponderosa Pine

Ponderosa pines thrive in dry, rocky soil. Their thick, reddish bark is fire-resistant. The tallest ponderosa pine in Oregon is found at La Pine State Park. It is 178 feet (54 m) tall and 342 inches (868 cm) in diameter.

10. Steller Sea Lion

The largest of the eared seals can swim up to 17 miles per hour (27 kmh). It's the only seal that can turn its flippers upside down to walk on land. More than two hundred live near Florence inside the largest sea cave system in North America.

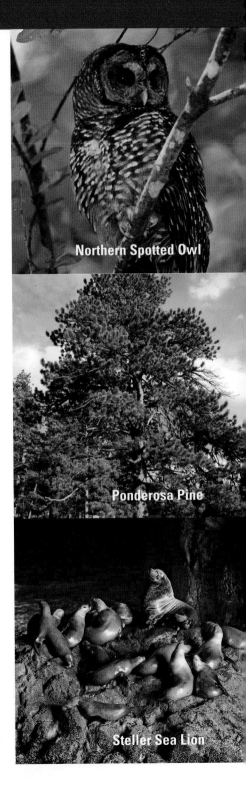

Northern Spotted Owl

Ponderosa Pine

Steller Sea Lion

Sacajawea serves as a translator between the Chinook and explorers Lewis and Clark in *Lewis and Clark on the Lower Columbia*, painted by Charles Russell in 1905.

From the Beginning

The first people who arrived in Oregon discovered, as did those who came later, that the region contained a wealth of native foods and natural resources. Scientific DNA tests reveal that the first inhabitants of Oregon came from north Asia. They were **nomads** who hunted large prehistoric animals such as woolly mammoths. It is believed that these hunters tracked the mammoths across a land bridge that connected what is now Alaska and Russia. New discoveries in an ancient cave at a national archeological site in Paisley, Oregon, have suggested that these first people living in Oregon may have been some of the earliest people to arrive in North America, possibly 14,000 years ago. About 7,500 years ago, the climate of the continent began changing and the area grew warmer; ice melted and lakes and rivers formed. New species of plants and animals began to flourish. With new plants to gather and new and smaller animals to hunt, the early nomads began settling down.

Native Americans of Oregon

The present day Native Americans of Oregon are descendants of these nomads. Since the first settlements, the native people have relied on the natural bounty of the region. Native Americans of the coast, such as the Tillamook or the Umpqua, feasted on salmon,

The Cayuse used dip nets to catch fish on the Columbia River.

shellfish, and sea mammals. They fashioned nets made from plants and placed them in the mouths of rivers to catch migrating salmon. Along the cliffs of the Columbia, Deschutes, and Rogue Rivers, Native American fishers built platforms that extended over the rushing water and dropped their nets. The fertile soil in the Willamette Valley and the Rogue River Valley provided other tribes, such as the Mollala and the Klamath, with wild fruits, nuts, and nutritious roots. The most important root was camas, which tastes like a sweet potato. People boiled camas to make a soup or dried the root into little cakes to store for winter. Tribes living in the many forests used trees to build homes, tools, and boats. The forest people hunted animals that lived in the woods, such as rabbit, deer, and elk. They crafted bows and arrows or wove rope nets to capture their prey. The groups that settled in the eastern section of present-day Oregon, such as the Paiute, hunted, fished, and gathered seeds for food, grasses for clothing, and found enough wood to provide bark and timber to build their homes and boats.

But because climate and geography varies from region to region, the natural resources and lifestyles of the native people also varied. Groups from different areas had different foods and tools, so the people developed a successful trading system. For example, coastal tribes traded sea shells, dried fish, and cedar baskets with tribes from central Oregon in exchange for animal hides, meat, and **obsidian** to make arrowheads and knives.

The First Europeans

It was not until the middle of the sixteenth century that Europeans reached the land that would one day be called Oregon. Some of the first Europeans were Spanish naval explorers who were looking for gold. They had heard rumors about secret cities filled with gold in North America. They sailed their ships northward from Mexico, looking for a river that would allow them to sail deeper into the North American continent. But when their ships reached the area around present-day Oregon, heavy storms kept them from getting any closer than the rugged Pacific shoreline.

Once the rumors of gold spread, many European countries became interested in the Pacific Northwest. Over the years, many countries sent ships along the coast, looking for rivers that would give them access inland. Settlers from Russia and Britain set up fur-trading posts in what is now Alaska and western Canada. Spanish settlers built outposts in the region that includes California. Each of these countries, at one time or another,

The Columbia River was named after Robert Gray's ship, the *Columbia Rediviva*.

The Native People

More than twenty major Native American tribes and many other smaller bands were living in Oregon when settlers arrived. Several tribal groups lived along the coast, such as the Coos, Siuslaw, Clatsop, Umpqua, and Tillamook. The Paiute lived on the plains of southeastern Oregon. The Mollala, Chinook, Bannock, Klamath, and other tribes lived in the mountains and valleys of the Cascades. The Nez Perce lived in the Wallowa Mountains, and the Cayuse, Walla Walla, and Umatilla lived near the Columbia River.

Coastal peoples enjoyed a temperate climate and a wealth of easy-to-harvest foods—berries, salmon, clams, and crabs. The Paiute hunted deer, elk, sheep, and rabbits, and fished for salmon. They collected seeds, berries, and roots and stored them for the winter. Winters were harsh and families took refuge in caves or built wood and sagebrush homes near hot springs. The Nez Perce and the Cayuse were skilled at raising horses and were expert hunters. Tribes living in the Cascades and along rivers hunted, trapped, and fished.

The 1850s were terrible times for Oregon's native people. American miners discovered gold and attacked native villages to gain control. Mining polluted the rivers. In 1850, Congress passed the Oregon Donation Act, which granted any white settler the right to claim 320 acres. The law was enacted to "leave the whole of the most desirable portion open to white settlers." The newcomers took over farmland and fishing grounds, and overhunted deer and elk. The native people were at risk of starvation. Settlers spread foreign diseases that infected and killed many Native Americans. Several tribes resisted. Eventually, the US army crushed all Native American opposition.

The US government signed peace treaties with some of the tribes and forced many Native Americans onto **reservations**. Today, there are nine

Study of a Umatilla Indian, Columbia River, 1905 was painted by Eanger Irving Couse.

federally recognized tribes: The Burns Paiute Tribe; the Confederated Tribes of Coos, Lower Umpqua & Siuslaw; Confederated Tribes of Grand Ronde; Confederated Tribes of Siletz; Confederated Tribes of the Umatilla; Confederated Tribes of Warm Springs; Coquille Indian Tribe; Cow Creek Band of Umpqua Indians; and the Klamath Tribes. Not every tribe was granted a reservation, so Native Americans in Oregon have created alliances within their reservations, such as the Confederated Tribes of the Umatilla Indian Reservation.

Spotlight on the Cayuse

Cayuse is pronounced "Kī-yüs." When French fur traders met the tribe, they called them the "Cailloux," meaning "Rock People," after the rocky cliffs in their homeland. The Cayuse were a small but powerful tribe. They were successful fishers, hunters, and horse breeders. Because of their wealth, they were active traders.

Distribution: The Cayuse belong to the Confederated Tribes of the Umatilla Indian Reservation, which occupies 271,000 square miles (700 sq km) in north central Oregon. The Cayuse have intermarried with other tribes of the confederation, which has a population of approximately 1,400 people.

Homes: The Cayuse stretched woven grass mats or animal skins on top of tall poles to make their houses. They packed up their mats when they moved to follow food sources but left the long, heavy poles behind.

Food: The Cayuse fished the Columbia River, building platforms over waterfalls and catching salmon in dip nets. They carved canoes to fish in smaller rivers. After salmon season, they gathered berries and dug roots to save for winter. In fall, the strongest horsemen of the tribe would trap and hunt in the mountains for deer, elk, and bear.

Clothing: The Cayuse wore little clothing in summer but dressed in deer, elk, or sheep skins in winter. They wore moccasins and leather leggings. Much of their clothing was decorated with fringe, feathers, beads, shells, and dyed cloth.

Art: The Cayuse believed in making everyday items beautiful. They decorated tools, pots, baskets, bags, and drums with colorful beadwork. They celebrated with dancing, singing, and drumming.

claimed the land of the Pacific Northwest. In 1775, the Spanish explorer Bruno de Heceta may have been the first European to find the mouth of the Columbia River. He claimed the surrounding region for Spain. Three years later, the British explorer Captain James Cook sailed up Oregon's coast. He landed in an area he named Cape Foulweather and discovered the thriving fur trade along the coast.

In 1788, Captain John Meares and Captain Robert Gray sailed from Boston to the Oregon coast. While their ships waited off the coast, Native American fur traders paddled their canoes to meet them. In 1792, Robert Gray successfully guided his ship into the same wild and dangerous river that Heceta had found. He sailed past the area John Meares had named Cape Disappointment and anchored in the calmer waters of the river's estuary. He was the first white explorer to actually enter the river. Gray named the river after his ship, the *Columbia Rediviva*. Other American explorers soon followed, and their discoveries helped support the United States's claim to the land that would become known as the Oregon Country.

The Lewis and Clark Expedition

In 1803, under President Thomas Jefferson's leadership, the United States bought a large area of land called the Louisiana Territory from France. This deal—called the Louisiana Purchase—gave the United States land that extended, east to west, from the Mississippi River to the Rocky Mountains. It included all or part of fourteen current US states. With this land, the country doubled in size. But Jefferson wanted the United States to extend from the Atlantic to the Pacific Oceans. He also wanted to find a water route from the eastern United States to the Pacific. To make part of that dream come true, he organized a group of explorers called the Corps of Discovery. Jefferson wanted this group to go west and learn as much about the land as possible, to make maps, and to befriend the native people. The Corps would travel by boat up the Missouri River to its farthest point and search for a water route that would continue to the Pacific Ocean. Jefferson appointed former army captain Meriwether Lewis to lead the group, and Lewis asked another former officer,

Glass Blower

Thirteen hundred years ago, the Newberry Crater near Bend spewed lava that formed obsidian, a sharp-edged volcanic glass. Native Americans from as far away as Canada traveled to the crater to quarry the obsidian to make tools and knives.

William Clark, to be a co-leader of what became known as the Lewis and Clark Expedition.

Lewis and Clark began their trip in 1804. By the late summer of 1805, they had traveled as far as they could up the Missouri River and reached the western boundary of the Louisiana Territory. They did not find a water route from there to the Pacific—no such route existed. Instead they traveled overland across the Rocky Mountains. Continuing west, they eventually journeyed by boat down the Snake and Columbia rivers, and by November 1805, they reached the mouth of the Columbia River and the Pacific Ocean. It had been a difficult journey and the men of the Corps of Discovery were relieved to have finally reached the Pacific. Patrick Gass, a member of the expedition, wrote that upon arriving at the Columbia River they saw "the country all round is level, rich and beautiful."

A statue honoring the Lewis and Clark Expedition was placed in Seaside.

The Corps built a log fort, which they named Fort Clatsop after a friendly local tribe, and spent the winter there. Sacagawea, a Shoshone woman, joined Lewis and Clark in North Dakota and traveled with them to the Oregon coast. She was an important addition to the Corps of Discovery for her knowledge of several native languages and for her expertise in identifying edible plants and fruits. At one point, one of the group's canoes capsized and she quickly rescued all the journals, medicines, and other valuables aboard. She remained with the Corps over their miserably wet winter at Fort Clatsop and later joined the Mandan tribe in North Dakota.

Lewis and Clark's trip proved to be a difficult but very important journey. As a result of their exploration, a path was forged that many settlers would soon follow. Although Lewis and Clark did not find the water route they were looking for, reports about their adventures—and about the natural resources of the region they had explored—inspired thousands of other people to move west.

Making an Oregon Trail Covered Wagon

Many people who settled Oregon got there by braving the long trip on the Oregon Trail. Here is how to build a model of a wagon like the ones they used.

What You Need

White construction paper

Scissors

39 Craft sticks

Glue

Two wood skewers

A box of cake or brownie mix

One plastic cup for tracing

A pencil or marker

What To Do

- Cut the front off of the cake or brownie mix box and set it aside. Remove the package of mix and give it to an adult. The top of the box will be the front of your wagon, and the bottom will be the back.

- Take eight craft sticks for each side of the wagon. Cut them down so when two are placed cut end to cut end they are the length of the sides of the box.

- Make four pairs of cut sticks so they make four boards for the sides of your wagon. Glue four pairs of boards to each side.

- Glue four pairs of boards to each end.

- Cut the ends off of six craft sticks and glue three pieces vertically to each side of the wagon.

- Glue one craft stick to the bottom of the front of your wagon as a pull.

- Cut the pointed end off each skewer. Glue one about 1 inch (2.5 cm) from the front and the other about 1 inch from the back of your wagon. These will be the axles.

- Trace four circles in the cardboard that you set aside. Cut them out for your wheels. Draw spokes on the wheels.

- Put a small hole in the center of each wheel and fit them over the skewers.

- Arch the white paper and glue it to the sides of your wagon. This makes the cover.

- You are now ready to travel the Oregon Trail.

Fur Trappers and Missionaries

Fur traders and trappers came to present-day Oregon from all over the United States, Canada (controlled by Great Britain in the early 1800s), and Russia. They were eager to hunt beavers and otters or trade with the Native Americans for pelts that could be sold for high prices. In 1811, John Jacob Astor built a permanent settlement at the mouth of the Columbia River. Astor was one of America's first millionaires. He bought pelts and sold them to Chinese traders in exchange for silk and porcelain, which he sold to wealthy Americans and Europeans. He named his company the Pacific Fur Company. This settlement became the town of Astoria. Yet survival was difficult. The waters were rough and ships sank, the weather was often stormy, and shipments of supplies were few. The War of 1812 broke out, and Astor and his men feared an attack by the British. They abandoned their fort and sold the company. The new owner, the Hudson Bay Company, established fur-trading outposts along the Columbia, Snake, and Willamette rivers, as well as in southeastern Oregon. The company encouraged trappers and traders to set up villages and farms and to build friendly relationships with Native Americans.

The **missionaries** came next. Missionaries traveled west hoping to convert the Native Americans to Christianity. It is possible that missionaries came to Oregon as a result of incorrect information. In 1832, a newspaper article reported that four members of the Nez Perce tribe had traveled to St. Louis, Missouri. They may have been looking for William Clark, who was working as the superintendent of Native American affairs in the Louisiana Territory. Many believe that the group had come in search of better tools and weapons, which they had seen used by members of the Lewis and Clark Expedition. The press reported, however, that they were looking for a new religion and wanted to become Christians. Once missionaries heard this, many of them made plans to travel west. In 1834, a minister named Jason Lee set up a permanent settlement in the Willamette Valley, near a village of former fur trappers by present-day Salem. Two years later, the

Customer's Always Right

In 1909, the Pendleton Woolen Mills started making blankets to trade with Native Americans. Unlike other blanket traders, they wanted to please their customers, so they wove blankets with bright colors and traditional Native American symbols. Pendleton blankets are highly prized to this day.

You can learn about life on the Oregon Trail at the Oregon Trail Interpretive Center near Baker City.

most famous of the missionaries, Marcus and Narcissa Whitman, set out for Oregon. They settled at the base of the Blue Mountains on the Walla Walla River among the Cayuse tribe. The Whitmans held church services, taught school, and practiced medicine. Their success encouraged many Americans to make the trip to Oregon along a route that became known as the Oregon Trail.

Oregon Trail

By the 1840s, people were pouring into the Oregon Country via the Oregon Trail. Thousands of wagon trains made the difficult journey, which for many of the pioneers began in Independence, Missouri, and following part of the route taken by Lewis and Clark, ended just south of Portland in the small town of Oregon City. The trip was more than

Champion Rider

Jackson Sundown was a Nez Perce rodeo rider who rode with Chief Joseph. In 1916, he won the World Championship at the Pendleton Round-Up. Afterwards, other rodeo riders withdrew from rodeos because they knew he would always win.

2,000 miles (3,200 km) long and often took four to five months to complete. The trail crossed three mountain ranges: the Rocky Mountains, the Blue Mountains, and the Cascades. Most people packed their belongings in large covered wagons, usually pulled by a team of oxen, and walked alongside. Many people died during the journey, but this did not stop others eager for a new life from developing "Oregon Fever" and venturing west.

Road to Statehood

In the early 1800s, both the United States and Great Britain claimed the Oregon Country, a region largely made up of the current states of Oregon, Washington, and Idaho, and most of the Canadian province of British Columbia. Under an 1818 treaty, the United States and Britain agreed to share the region. In 1831, the United States and Spain, which controlled California, established the present day southern border of Oregon. But as more and more Americans traveled the Oregon Trail and settled in the Oregon Territory, the US government claimed that the United States should not share control of the area with Britain. In 1846, the two nations reached a compromise. Britain gave up its claim to land south of what is now the northern border of Washington State, and the United States gave up its claim to the land north of that border.

With the dispute over control of the region resolved, many settlers in what is now Oregon wanted their new homeland to become a state. As a step in that direction, in 1848, Congress passed a measure, which was signed by President James K. Polk, establishing the Oregon Territory. The territory originally included the land that would eventually become the states of Oregon, Washington, and Idaho, as well as parts of Montana and Wyoming.

Two years later, Congress passed the Oregon Donation Land Act. This law gave 320 acres (120 hectares) of free land to anyone who promised to plant crops

Missionary Narcissa Whitman was killed with her husband, Marcus, by Cayuse warriors after a misunderstanding.

10 KEY CITIES

Portland

1. Portland: population 583,776

Portland is located along the Willamette and Columbia Rivers. Nicknamed the "City of Roses" for its many gardens, Portland is a politically liberal home to a colorful and sometimes quirky variety of shops, galleries, cafes, bookstores, restaurants, music venues, parks, and more.

2. Eugene: population 156,185

Eugene is home to the University of Oregon. Located along the tree-lined banks of the McKenzie and Willamette rivers, Eugene is known for its many arts and cultural events as well as for numerous recreational opportunities.

3. Salem: population 154,637

Salem is the state capital and lies along the Willamette River in the Willamette Valley. The town's original name, "Chemekta," meant "meeting or resting place." The city has many historic buildings, including a gilded pioneer statue atop the capitol dome.

4. Gresham: population 105,594

Gresham lies just east of Portland near a section of the Columbia River gorge. It is a suburban shopping hub. A favorite destination is the Gresham Pioneer Museum.

5. Hillsboro: population 91,611

Hillsboro is in the Tualatin Valley along the Tualatin River. Despite its name, Hillsboro is not very hilly. Rather, it is flat and excellent for farming. Today, Hillsboro is the heart of the "Silicon Forest," where many technology and computer-related manufacturers are located.

Salem

6. Beaverton: population 89,803

Beaverton lies west of Portland and is connected by a popular light rail system called "MAX." It is home to the region's "Silicon Forest," where many technology companies operate.

7. Bend: population 76,639

Situated on the banks of the Deschutes River and at the base of Mount Bachelor, Bend is one of the state's fastest-growing cities. Sunshine and many outdoor recreation activities appeal to tourists and residents alike.

8. Medford: population 74,907

Medford lies in the Rogue River Valley. When the railroad between San Francisco and Portland was built in the 1880s, Medford became a trade center. Famous companies such as Harry & David foods and Jackson & Perkins Seed Company are located in Medford today.

9. Springfield: population 59,403

Filbert nut orchards surround Springfield. It is separated from Eugene by Interstate 5 to form a metropolitan area. Cartoonist Matt Groening, who created the animated TV series *The Simpsons*, said that he named his characters' hometown after Springfield, Oregon.

10. Corvallis: population 54,462

Corvallis is set in the middle of the Willamette Valley, along the banks of the Willamette River. The area is surrounded by grass-seed fields, which produce most of the nation's grass seed. Corvallis is home to Oregon State University, a major agricultural research center.

Beaverton

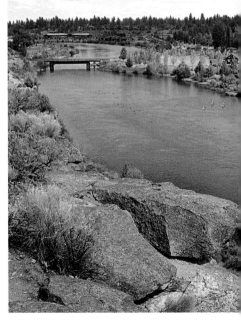

Bend

Chief Joseph of the Nez Perce vows never to fight again.

on it. The offer of free land brought a new wave of people to Oregon. In 1851, gold was discovered in southern and eastern Oregon. By the 1860s, Oregon—like California before it—experienced a gold rush.

With all these trappers, missionaries, settlers, and gold miners rushing into Oregon, the Native American population began to suffer. In 1805, it was estimated that more than forty thousand Native Americans lived in the region. Their numbers were decreasing, however. The trappers and other new residents were hunting and killing animals that the Native Americans had once relied on for food. The settlers were claiming land that had belonged to the Native Americans. The miners polluted the waters when they dug for gold, killing fish and making the water unsafe to drink.

White people also carried diseases, such as smallpox and measles, to which the Native Americans had never been exposed and had no natural immunity. In 1847, at the Whitman mission, a measles epidemic struck the white children and Cayuse children alike. The white children survived, but the Cayuse children died. The Cayuse believed the deaths were an attempt by the Whitmans to steal their land to make room for the new white settlers. A group of Cayuse warriors attacked the mission buildings, killing the Whitmans and twelve other white settlers. A white militia responded by attacking some Cayuse who had not been involved in the first incident. The conflict escalated into the Cayuse War, which lasted until 1850. There were also tensions between settlers and other tribes. More wars followed, including the Rogue River War of 1855–1856. Native Americans were not able to drive out the white settlers, but they fought to protect and reclaim their land. Federal troops became involved, and many Native Americans were moved to reservations.

By 1857, the Oregon Territory had been divided in two: a smaller Oregon Territory and a separate Washington Territory. A convention was called to write a state constitution for Oregon. Two years later, on February 14, 1859, Oregon (with its present boundaries) became the thirty-third state.

Conflicts between white settlers and tribal groups persisted after statehood. In 1877, the US Army ordered Chief Joseph—leader of the Nez Perce—to take his people from their traditional home in eastern Oregon to a reservation in present-day Idaho. Angered, Nez Perce warriors raided a settlement and killed several whites. Chief Joseph tried to escape by leading his people toward Canada, but the US troops followed them and several battles were fought. The band of Nez Perce was no match for the US Army and so in the bitter cold, many of the Nez Perce froze or starved to death. With so much loss, Chief Joseph surrendered, saying, "I am tired. My heart is sick and sad. From where the sun now stands I will fight no more forever." Army troops forced the chief and his small remaining band to a reservation in present-day Oklahoma, where many died from disease. By the end of the 1800s, fewer than ten thousand Native Americans remained in the state.

Modern Times and Growing Pains

When a transcontinental railroad line reached Oregon in the 1880s—enabling people to go from the eastern United States to Oregon by train—travel to the new state became

Oregon's population increased after the transcontinental railroad reached the state in the 1880s.

much easier. The number of people living in Oregon grew rapidly. Between 1900 and 1910, for instance, Portland's population grew from about ninety thousand to more than two hundred thousand. Some of the people who arrived in Oregon during this time were not as interested in being farmers or ranchers as the settlers who had come before them. Many of these new residents were used to living in cities, so they developed Oregon's cities instead, building new stores and other types

City of Firsts

In 1844, Oregon City was the first city incorporated west of the Mississippi River. In 1851, it became the first capital of the Oregon Territory. It also had the only real estate office west of the Rockies where settlers could stake their homestead claims.

of businesses. The capital of Salem was named after Salem, Massachusetts. Portland was named after Portland, Maine, after a coin toss between a man from Maine and a man from Massachusetts, who wanted to name the new city Boston. The man from Maine won the coin toss and the coin he used is on display at the Oregon Historical Society in Portland.

The railroad also provided a way of transporting goods from Oregon to other parts of the nation. Wheat and lumber grown in Oregon could now be shipped east. This meant that more people could buy these products, and Oregon's economy began to grow. Factories were built in Oregon's cities, creating jobs for many residents.

Hard times hit Oregon—and the rest of the nation—with the **Great Depression**. Starting in 1929, this was a period of time when the country's economy was in terrible shape. Banks and businesses closed, and many people lost their jobs and their homes. The federal government established programs to help the unemployed find work while also rebuilding the country. Workers were hired for such projects as constructing roads, logging forests, and building dams. Many Oregonians helped build the Bonneville Dam, which was completed in 1938. By taming the current of the Columbia River, the dam

The Bonneville Dam was completed in 1938, near the end of the Great Depression.

helped create electric power for homes and businesses throughout the Pacific Northwest. The reservoir behind the dam provided irrigation water for farms. The availability of inexpensive electricity also helped to make Portland one of the nation's major shipbuilding centers.

World War II began in Europe in 1939, with the United States joining the war in December 1941, after Japan attacked the US naval base at Pearl Harbor, Hawaii. In June 1942, a Japanese submarine fired shells on Fort Stevens, at the mouth of the Columbia River on the Oregon side. It was the only time during World War II that there was hostile shelling of a military base on the US mainland. Factories needed workers to make supplies for the war effort. Oregon's urban areas became important manufacturing centers for war materials, and the state's farms helped supply the troops with food. The war helped improve the US economy.

After World War II ended, Oregon entered a period of relative prosperity. There was increased demand for the state's lumber and beef, and electricity was brought to remote areas. As a result of the tapping of new water sources, land that had once been dry could now be planted. New highway construction helped bring tourists to see the state's wonders. There were challenges, however, for some people. Small farmers faced increased competition from larger farms whose owners could afford new machinery and chemicals for their crops. The overall rural farm population dropped, causing hardships for small towns.

It was also during the 1950s and 1960s that Oregonians began to notice that some of their industries were causing great environmental damage. Factories had turned the Willamette River into a sewer, contaminating the water with their waste. In other places, entire mountainsides had been stripped of trees by the lumber industry. This caused dangerous mudslides that clogged rivers and damaged homes. Oregonians became determined to make their state healthy again. Oregon enacted laws to protect and clean up the environment. By the 1970s, Oregon became the state with the most laws protecting animals and other natural resources. The tradition continues today.

In Their Own Words

"I honor the memory of those brave settlers of Oregon ... Theirs was a quest for new horizons, for new beginnings. For a new homeland. They rode. They walked. They starved. They foraged. And they died. But they kept their eyes westward. They gave us Oregon."
–Governor Barbara Roberts, 1991

Oregonians have worked hard to protect and restore the environment.

Oregon Today

Oregon is rich in natural resources. Those resources, however, need protection and **conservation**. Today, the people of Oregon know that they cannot overfish their rivers or the fish will become endangered. They know that if too many forests are cleared by the logging industry, this clearing will destroy plant and animal habitats and cause mudslides. Oregonians are committed to keeping their state healthy and clean. This not only makes Oregon a fine place to live, it also attracts people from other states who enjoy visiting Oregon's beaches, mountains, and deserts. The money that tourists spend helps to create jobs.

Although Oregon is changing, in many ways it also remains the same. Just as in the pioneer days, people from all over the nation still hear that Oregon is a desirable place to live. In fact, it is among the fastest growing states in the nation, with its diverse population increasing 12 percent between 2000 and 2010. The air quality is good. The temperatures are mild.

In Their Own Words

"We come from the land. We are the earth, we are the land. The others occupy the land. When you destroy the salmon, you destroy me. The salmon made a commitment to return and to give life."
—Louie Dick, Jr., Confederated Tribes of the Umatilla Indian Reservation

And the natural environment offers many exciting outdoor adventures. Traveling to Oregon is far easier than it was hundreds of years ago, and when people come to the state, they still find a land of green rolling hills and a wonderful place to establish a new home.

10 KEY DATES IN STATE HISTORY

1. **11,500 BCE**

The first people arrive in what is now Oregon. They were nomads who had crossed a land bridge between Russia and Alaska to follow and hunt large mammals.

2. **May 11, 1792**

American Robert Gray guides his ship into the Columbia River, naming the river after his ship, *Rediviva Columbia*, and claiming the Oregon Country for the United States.

3. **1843**

Pioneers begin a major migration to the Oregon Country along the Oregon Trail, walking beside oxen-pulled covered wagons packed with their belongings.

4. **August 14, 1848**

The US Congress establishes the Oregon Territory, an area that includes what is today Oregon, Idaho, Washington State, and western Montana.

5. **February 14, 1859**

Oregon becomes the thirty-third state. It enters the Union with a constitution that prohibits slavery, but bans African Americans from living in the state.

6. **October 5, 1877**

Chief Joseph surrenders to the US Army after a march of 1,400 miles (2,253 km) and many battles in an attempt to reach Canada. His band of seven hundred Nez Perce had been ordered to relocate to Idaho.

7. **June 6, 1938**

The Bonneville dam is completed, providing electricity for homes and businesses and irrigation for farms.

8. **November 6, 1990**

Barbara Roberts is elected the first female governor. The former majority leader in the Oregon House of Representatives also served two terms as the Oregon Secretary of State.

9. **July 13, 2002**

Biscuit Creek wildfire, set by lightning strikes, burns more than 500,000 acres (202,343 ha) of wilderness in the Siskiyou National Forest.

10. **October 28, 2013**

The governor of Oregon signs an agreement with California, Washington, and British Columbia, Canada, to reduce greenhouse gases.

Mount Hood provides snowboarding and other recreational opportunities popular among residents of Oregon.

The People

3

The people who have lived in Oregon—from the earliest inhabitants thousands of years ago to the people currently living in the state—have shown an independent spirit and an appreciation for the natural beauty and bounty of their land. Most certainly, the region's natural resources first drew people to settle in the state and have since given people a livelihood and a sense of well-being.

Today, Oregonians share many of the same values, such as a clean environment and a belief in justice for all, but it was not always the case. Groups of people came to Oregon in waves—the early nomads, the fur traders and trappers, missionaries, pioneers, miners, railroad and business people, fishers, loggers, and laborers. And as each new group arrived, society changed.

The very first immigrants who came to Oregon, after the Native people, were the trappers and traders who were called "mountain men." They respected the Native Americans. They traded for pelts with the Native Americans, who were happy to receive European goods in return. The mountain men, mostly British and French, were interested in the native people's culture and many had Native American wives. They learned Native American languages and developed a trading language that all people could understand. The language was called "Chinook," named after a successful trading tribe. When new waves of immigrants arrived, the mountain men served as translators for them.

Who Oregonians Are

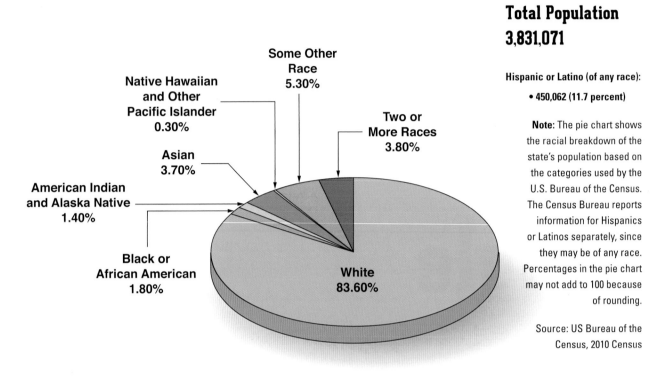

Total Population
3,831,071

Some Other Race 5.30%

Native Hawaiian and Other Pacific Islander 0.30%

Asian 3.70%

American Indian and Alaska Native 1.40%

Black or African American 1.80%

Two or More Races 3.80%

White 83.60%

Hispanic or Latino (of any race):

• 450,062 (11.7 percent)

Note: The pie chart shows the racial breakdown of the state's population based on the categories used by the U.S. Bureau of the Census. The Census Bureau reports information for Hispanics or Latinos separately, since they may be of any race. Percentages in the pie chart may not add to 100 because of rounding.

Source: US Bureau of the Census, 2010 Census

Relationships Soured

After the first encounter between European Americans and Native Americans, relationships worsened. The next wave—white missionaries—began by serving the native people. They taught, practiced medicine, and preached Christianity to them and fed them. However, they soon turned to serving the incoming white pioneers. After the Whitman mission massacre, years of violent conflict followed. With settlers armed with guns and metal knives, and Native Americans with war clubs and arrows, people no longer trusted one another.

The tension got worse when the miners arrived in the next wave. The miners were tough and often greedy. They took over land and laid waste to the environment.

The next to arrive were the people who came to make lots of money. Many took advantage of both the Native Americans and the white settlers. They were railroad men, land dealers, and other, sometimes corrupt, businessmen. As American business interests became more profitable, government army troops were sent to establish forts to protect trade and commerce. The soldiers brought their aides and their families with them. Farms and towns expanded.

Soon, whites outnumbered the Native Americans. As Oregon continued to prosper, more white immigrants came—Greeks to work on the railroads, Swedes to work in lumber mills, and Norwegians and Finns to take part in the fishing industry. Oregon's many farmers came from Germany, Denmark, Ireland, and Italy. In eastern Oregon, Basque sheepherders established ranches.

New Waves

Hawaiian Islanders were among the first non-white immigrants to Oregon. They came on British trading ships and began to work for fur trading companies. They were skillful at navigating canoes and worked at transporting goods along the Columbia River.

Chinese immigrants arrived in the 1850s. They were farmers who had left their homes because of famine and war.

The Klamath lived in southern Oregon near Klamath Lake.

They came hoping to find jobs and save money to return home. Railroad companies recognized how willing Chinese men were to work hard for long hours and little pay. They sent agents to China as well as Japan to hire workers to build the railroads. As the economy grew, more laborers were needed for difficult low-wage jobs such as fish-packing or logging. Many of the people hired for these jobs were Chinese and Japanese. Asian immigrants faced a great deal of discrimination. They were forced to live apart from the whites in neighborhoods called "Chinatowns." By 1900, Portland had the second-largest Chinese immigrant community in the United States (after San Francisco, California).

In 1942, during World War II, President Franklin Roosevelt ordered all Japanese on the West Coast to return to Japan and all Japanese Americans to be relocated to internment camps. After the war, some Japanese Americans returned to Oregon, but others lost all they owned and moved elsewhere. Later, other Asian people immigrated to

1. Carrie Brownstein

Carrie Brownstein was born in Seattle but moved to Portland. She is a guitar player, singer, actress, and comedian. She founded the band Sleater-Kinney. She and Fred Armisen worked on the television sketch comedy show *Saturday Night Live* before creating the television comedy series *Portlandia*.

Carrie Brownstein

Ty Burrell

Ann Curry

2. Ty Burrell

Ty Burrell was born in Grants Pass and graduated from Southern Oregon University in Ashland in 1993. He worked at the Oregon Shakespeare Festival before becoming a television and movie actor. He plays the father, Phil Dunphy, on the television show *Modern Family*.

3. Chief Joseph

Chief Joseph of the Nez Perce was born in the Wallowa Valley around 1840. After the US government ordered his tribe out of Oregon, he led a failed escape to Canada in the bitter cold.

4. Beverly Cleary

Born in McMinnville in 1916, Beverly Cleary grew up on a farm in Yamhill. She has won numerous awards for her children's books, including a Newbery Medal for *Dear Mr. Henshaw*.

5. Ann Curry

Ann Curry was born in 1956 in Guam but grew up in Ashland. She graduated with a journalism degree from the University of Oregon and worked as television news reporter in Medford and Portland. She has won many awards, including Emmy awards, as a reporter for NBC news.

OREGON ★ ★ ★ ★ ★

6. Matt Groening

Matt Groening was born in Portland in 1954. His father was a cartoonist who taught him how to draw. His animated cartoon series, *The Simpsons*, started on television in 1990 and is the longest running television show ever.

7. Phil Knight

Phil Knight was born in 1938 in Portland. He graduated from the University of Oregon, where he ran track. He and his former coach, Bill Bowerman, started what would become Nike. He has donated millions of dollars to Oregon schools.

8. Ursula Le Guin

Ursula Le Guin lives in Portland and has written numerous books, including the *Earthsea Cycle* and the Catwings series. She has received several awards, including the National Book Award for Children's Books (for *The Farthest Shore*), for fantasy and science fiction.

9. Linus Pauling

Linus Pauling was born in Portland in 1901. He received degrees from Oregon State College and the California Institute of Technology. He won the Nobel Prize in Chemistry in 1954. He became an anti-war activist and was awarded the Nobel Peace Prize in 1962.

10. Ahmad Rashad

Born Robert Moore in Portland in 1949, he changed his name in 1972. He set records while playing football at the University of Oregon and starred in the National Football League. He is a sportscaster and producer for NBC.

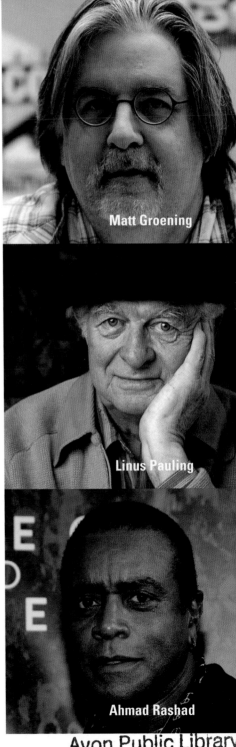

Matt Groening

Linus Pauling

Ahmad Rashad

Oregon, many to escape wars in their homelands—Korea, Vietnam, Cambodia, Laos, Thailand, and the Philippines. Today, nearly 5 percent of Oregonians are of Asian or Pacific Islander descent.

Few African Americans immigrated to Oregon. One who did was Moses Harris, a fur trapper and mountain man, who later became a guide on the Oregon Trail. Another who did was Louis Southworth, who had been born a slave, traveled the Oregon Trail and earned his living first as a musician in the gold mining camps. He became a homesteader and donated some of his land for a school.

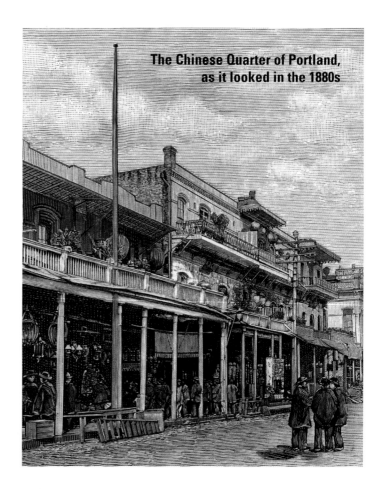

The Chinese Quarter of Portland, as it looked in the 1880s

Exclusion Laws

In the mid-nineteenth century, the United States was made up of free states and slave-owning states. White pioneers in Oregon came from the Midwest and few were slave-owners, but they lived near, and competed with, farmers who did not have to pay the enslaved people who worked for them. White settlers feared if slavery were allowed in Oregon Country, it would harm their livelihoods. So in 1843, white settlers voted to ban slavery, but they also demanded that all African Americans leave Oregon Country. Although punishment for defying the law was whipping or hard labor, the law was not often enforced.

However, on August 20, 1851, a businessman named Jacob Vanderpool, who owned a saloon, restaurant, and boarding house, became the first African American known to have been banished from Oregon because of his race. For several decades, African Americans were not allowed to own property or sign legal contracts. This type of law is called an exclusion law. When Oregon was accepted into the union as a free state, it was the only one to have exclusion laws in its constitution. These laws were not repealed until 1927.

Even after Congress abolished slavery in 1865, there were only a few African-American homesteaders in Oregon. During World War II, however, African Americans moved to Portland to build navy ships and military tanks and weapons. The population of African Americans in Oregon at that time tripled. Still, today the percentage of the population in Oregon that is African-American is low (2 percent) compared to the rest of the nation (12 percent).

Hispanics—people whose origins are from Spanish-speaking countries—are Oregon's largest ethnic minority group. There were Mexican immigrants in Oregon before the pioneers. In the 1800s, Mexicans came to Oregon to work as cowboys or to run mule trains that brought supplies to the army. Many stayed to farm. During World War II, many young Oregonians were called to serve in the military, leaving a shortage of people available to work on farms. Mexican workers came to Oregon to help harvest the much-needed crops. Many stayed to start farms and businesses, or joined the military. In the 1970s and 1980s, many Central Americans immigrated to Oregon, escaping war and poverty in their home countries. Hispanic people are Oregon's fastest-growing community.

McCants Stewart was Oregon's first African-American lawyer, but his law practice suffered because whites did not hire black attorneys.

Education

Since the first public school was opened in 1833, Oregonians have placed a strong importance on education. Despite the small populations and the miles between neighbors in rural areas, schools and colleges were created. Today, more than 550,000 students are enrolled in grades kindergarten through twelve in Oregon's public schools. The state recently passed laws allowing bilingual (Spanish and English) education in public schools. There are several public elementary and high schools located on Native American reservations that focus on understanding native culture and language. In 2010, during a time of economic decline, Oregonians nonetheless voted to increase taxes to help improve public schools.

In 1842, Willamette University was established in Portland, and it is the oldest university in the western United States. Oregon has more than twenty colleges and universities, numerous community colleges, as well as technical, medical, and art schools. Large universities include the University of Oregon in Eugene, Portland State University in Portland, and Oregon State University in Corvallis. The state also has many private colleges and universities. One is Reed College, founded in 1908 in Portland, which is regarded as one of the most challenging colleges in the United States. Approximately 28 percent of Oregonians have a college bachelor's degree, which is about the national average. The state has set a goal of raising that figure to 40 percent by the year 2025.

Pastimes

Oregonians share their many talents with each other, enjoying a creative array of art, music, literature, food, festivals, and sports. Portland, Eugene, Ashland, and Cannon Beach are known for their art museums, galleries, restaurants, theaters, and concerts. Small towns and communities also enjoy the arts. Many have specialty festivals, celebrating their heritage or their livelihood. Among them are the Chief Joseph Days Rodeo and the Scandinavian Festival in the town of Junction City, where more than one hundred thousand people show up each year.

For the Little People

Portland's Mill Ends Park is only 24 inches [60 cm] wide; the smallest city park in the world. Created in 1948 as a "home for leprechauns," it is the heart of St. Patrick's Day celebrations. People leave tiny gifts, such as a swimming pool for leprechauns, a diving board for butterflies, and a miniature Ferris wheel.

In the Cascade Mountains, the city of Ashland hosts the famous, months-long Oregon Shakespeare Festival. Oregonians are also avid readers. There are many bookstores throughout the state. Powell's bookstore in Portland is the largest independent bookstore in the world. Shoppers use maps to find their way around the store.

Oregonians also share a love of sports. Together they cheer the Portland Trailblazers professional basketball team, as well as the Portland Timbers soccer team. However, most Oregonians take sides when it comes to college sports, especially football. People either root for the Oregon State Beavers or the University of Oregon Ducks. Every fall, the two teams play one another in a game that they call "The Civil War."

Oregonians enjoy being outdoors, and they are fortunate to have many recreational options. They can go mountain biking, fishing, camping, hiking, horseback riding, beach-combing, skiing, or jogging, or they can tend a rose garden. It is not only people living in rural areas who spend much of their time outdoors. City dwellers say access to the outdoors is the reason they live in Oregon. Oregonians enjoy many water sports such as swimming, river rafting, kayaking, and sailing.

One water sport Oregon is well known for is windsurfing. All year long, the small city of Hood River, which is located on the

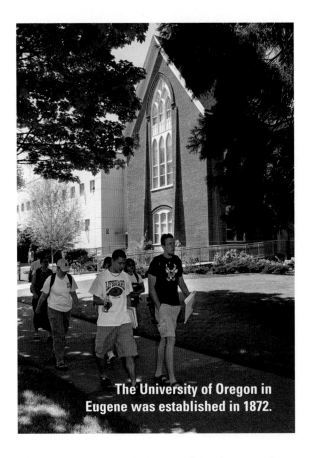

The University of Oregon in Eugene was established in 1872.

cliffs above the Columbia Gorge, attracts windsurfers from around the world. The wind is very strong as it rips down the gorge and Hood River is often called the "Windsurfing Capital of the World." The Rogue and Deschutes Rivers also attract outdoor enthusiasts. Their rushing, clear waters contain many waterfalls and rapids that challenge and excite kayakers and river rafters.

There are more than two hundred parks inside the city limits of Portland, including a world famous rose garden, a Japanese garden, and a zoo. The Lan Su Chinese Garden is a beautiful Ming Dynasty–style garden near downtown. There is a park along the Willamette River called Forest Park, which has 5,156 acres (2,086 ha) of old growth trees and 70 miles (112 km) of trails.

Oregonians like their great outdoors, their way of life, and their relatively small population. In the 1970s and 1980s, outsiders were often discouraged from moving to Oregon. At one point, the well-liked governor, Tom McCall, joked by saying, "Please come visit Oregon, but for heaven's sake, don't stay!" Despite the discouraging words, people know Oregon is a very desirable place to live. And even during the economic hard times in the 2000s, people continued to move to Oregon. As a matter of fact, in 2013, Oregon was the number one destination among people who moved from one state to another.

1. Oregon Shakespeare Festival

Since 1935, Ashland has hosted this festival, with both indoor and outdoor theaters. Each year, more than one hundred thousand people attend performances of plays and music. The festival runs from February to October.

2. Asian Kite Festival

The Asian Kite Festival in Eugene takes place in the windy month of March. Besides kite-making classes, exhibits, and kite flying competitions there are musicians, dancers, and artists, such as Japanese Taiko drummers and Chinese Lion Dancers.

3. America's Global Village Festival

America's Global Village Festival takes place in Ontario, Oregon in June. Many of Oregon's ethnic groups are represented in separate "villages"—each of which displays music, traditional crafts, food, and dance of ethnic groups.

4. Oregon Winterfest

Held in Bend, near Mount Bachelor, the Winterfest includes ice-carving competitions, snowman building contests, and a polar bear plunge. The popular Rail Jam event is a snowboard competition for which fifty truckloads of snow are formed into a snowboard course in the center of town.

5. Cannon Beach Sandcastle Contest

This sandcastle building contest, held in June, is the largest in the Northwest. Teams consist of sculptors and people who carry buckets of water and sand to them. The spectacular castles are judged just before the tide washes them away.

Oregon Shakespeare Festival

Cannon Beach Sandcastle Festival

6. John Scharff Migratory Bird Festival

In April, people gather at the Malheur National Wildlife Refuge in Burns to witness the arrival of thousands of migratory birds from their winter breeding grounds. At this vast wetlands surrounded by desert, birders can watch songbirds, wading birds, raptors, and cranes.

7. Oregon Country Fair

Nearly fifty years ago, the Oregon Country Fair in Veneta was called the Renaissance Faire. Visitors wore period costumes. Today, fair-goers still wear costumes, but they are often outlandish. Musicians, craftspeople, food vendors, and entertainers join to create a festival people call "magical."

8. Oregon State Fair

In late August, Oregon celebrates with art, music, concerts, and events in Salem. There are horseback riding, livestock-raising, and small animal (rabbits, chickens, birds) competitions. One day, the *Día de la Familia*, is devoted to Hispanic heritage.

9. Pendleton Round-Up

Since 1910, thousands of people have attended the Pendleton Round-Up each September. They come to watch parades, Wild West pageants, concerts, bareback riding, steer roping, bull riding, barrel racing, and Native American foot races.

10. Portland Rose Festival

The Portland Rose Festival attracts visitors each summer from around the world. Visitors enjoy the Floral Parade, fireworks, crafts, music, and a nighttime starlight parade.

Oregon Country Fair

Pendleton Round-Up

Oregon State Capitol State Park sports beautiful blooms in the spring.

How the Government Works

4

In the early 1800s, there was no single set of laws governing the Oregon Country. Native Americans governed themselves under tribal laws. Canadian fur trappers and traders, as well as other settlers from Canada, then controlled by Great Britain, considered themselves governed by British law. By the 1840s, more of the Oregon Country's population consisted of people who had come from, or whose families had come from, the eastern United States. In 1843, a group of 102 American settlers came together and decided to set up a provisional (temporary) government. This group of settlers also selected a committee to write a constitution. The constitution was called the Organic Act, and when it was adopted on July 5, the Provisional Government of Oregon was born.

The Provisional Government had the same basic form as the government of the United States. It had an executive branch, a legislature, and a judicial system. The executive branch was a committee of three instead of an individual. However, this was not successful, so a governor was appointed.

Oregon became a US territory in 1848. The first territorial governors were appointed by the president of the United States. In 1857, Oregon's present-day constitution was adopted and in 1858, "Honest John" Whiteaker became the first governor of the Oregon Territory elected by the people.

Branches of Government

Executive

The governor of Oregon serves as the head of the executive branch. The governor is elected to a four-year term and cannot serve more than two terms. He or she is responsible for appointing the heads of many agencies, proposing the state budget, and approving or rejecting proposed laws. Other elected positions in the executive branch are the attorney general, the secretary of state, the commissioner of labor and industries, the superintendent of public instruction, and the treasurer.

The Oregon Pioneer statue sits on top of the Capitol Building in Salem.

Legislative

The legislative branch of government makes the laws. The Oregon legislature is made up of two houses (or chambers)—the state Senate and the state House of Representatives. There are thirty senators and sixty representatives. Senators are elected to four-year terms and representatives to two-year terms. There are no limits to the number of terms that legislators can serve.

Judicial

The judicial branch is responsible for seeing that the laws are followed and that state laws do not violate the Oregon constitution. The Supreme Court is the highest court in the state. There are seven Supreme Court justices. Ten judges serve on the next highest court, the Court of Appeals. Most trials are held in the circuit courts. Circuit court decisions can be appealed to the Court of Appeals, and sometimes the Supreme Court. All judges are elected to a six-year term. Oregon also has a tax court. It hears appeals on personal income taxes, corporate excise taxes, and property taxes, among other things. An excise tax is paid when someone buys a specific good, such as gasoline. The tax is usually included in the price of that good.

Local Government

Oregon also has local governments that serve its cities and counties. Oregon's cities use a form of home rule, which means each city has the right to choose its own form of government. The people of Portland elect a mayor, four commissioners, and an auditor to guide their city. In other cities, a city manager or mayor and a council take care of government affairs. Each of Oregon's thirty-six counties also has its own government. In each county, elected members work together on a board of commissioners.

How a Bill Becomes a Law

All of Oregon's laws begin with an idea. This idea can come from just about anyone: an ordinary citizen, a group of citizens or an organization, a member of the state legislature, or the governor, to name just a few possibilities. A proposed law that is considered in the legislature is called a bill. Bills may create new laws, remove or amend (change) old laws, or provide money for special projects. In order for a bill to become a law, it must go through many different steps. First, the idea (if it does not originate with a member of the legislature) is given to either a state senator or representative, who must sponsor the bill, or accept responsibility for it. If the bill is sponsored by a senator, then it is first worked on in the Senate. If it is sponsored by a representative, then it is first worked on in the House of Representatives.

Elected officials in Portland meet in City Hall.

The senator or representative sponsoring the bill gives it to lawyers in the Legislative Counsel office, where it is written in correct legal language. Then the chief clerk of the Senate or House assigns the bill a special number. Before it returns to the Senate or the House, it is printed and read one more time by the lawyers.

A mural depicting people learning that Oregon has become a state is placed at the front of the state senate chamber.

The bill is then returned to either the Senate or the House for its first official reading. After the senators or representatives have all heard it, the bill is sent to a committee by the Speaker of the House or the President of the Senate. The members of the committee consider the bill, and the committee may hold hearings to get reactions to the bill from members of the public and from organizations that may be affected by the bill. If the committee votes to pass the bill, it is returned to where it started—either the Senate or the House—and read again. Committee members might have changed the bill when they were considering it, so everyone must be brought up to date on those amendments, or changes. The bill is then read for the third time, and this time the members of the Senate or House vote on it. In order to pass, the bill must receive at least thirty-one votes in the House or sixteen votes in the Senate.

A bill that has passed in one chamber then goes to the other chamber, where the whole process of being considered is repeated. Sometimes, the second chamber makes changes to the bill before passing it. Then, a group made up of members from both chambers—called a conference committee—must arrive at a final version of the bill. Both the Senate and the House must vote to accept the bill's final version.

After a bill has passed in both the Senate and the House in exactly the same form, it is sent to the governor. If the governor signs it, the bill becomes law. The governor also has the power to veto, or reject, the bill. If this happens, the Senate and the House members can vote for it again. If two-thirds of the members of the Senate and the House vote in favor of the bill, they can override the governor's veto, and the bill becomes a law.

Not all state laws have to be passed by the legislature. One of the most interesting things about Oregon's government is what is called the Oregon System. Under the Oregon System, citizens can play a major role in making laws and changing the state constitution through what is called the **initiative** process. If citizens who want a new law or a constitutional change gather a specific number of signatures from Oregon voters, their idea—the initiative—will be put to a vote in a general election. This means that everyone in the state can vote on the initiative. If it gets a majority vote, it becomes a state law or constitutional amendment.

Oregon in the Federal Government

Like all states, Oregon is represented in the US Congress in Washington, DC. Each state has two senators in the US Senate. The number of members each state has in the US House of Representatives is determined by the state's population. States that have larger populations have more members. California has the most, with fifty-three. Some states have only one. In 2014, Oregon had five representatives.

Silly Laws

In the early 1900s, Klamath Falls's sidewalks were wooden boardwalks. Snakes often poked their heads up through the boards and passers-by would kick their heads off, leaving the bodies to rot and create a foul odor. So, it is illegal in Klamath Falls to knock the heads off of snakes when walking on the sidewalk.

POLITICAL FIGURES
FROM OREGON

★ Mark Hatfield: United States Senator, 1967-1997

Mark Hatfield was a professor, state congressman, senator, and governor who later became a respected US Senate leader. As a former Navy officer, he witnessed the destruction caused in World War II and Vietnam. During his Senate career he opposed war and focused on combating world hunger, poverty, and illness.

★ Tom McCall: Governor, 1967-1975

Tom McCall was an environmentalist who supported laws such as protecting the coastal beaches from development and creating the nation's first bottle-deposit bill, aimed at reducing litter. Portland's McCall Waterfront Park, along the Willamette River, honors him as the person responsible for tearing down a freeway to create the park.

★ Barbara Roberts: Governor, 1991-1995

Barbara Roberts was the first female majority leader of the state House of Representatives and went on to be the first female governor. She was an advocate for the people, helping develop the Oregon Health Plan, increasing funding for Head Start, and supporting the development of affordable housing for the poor.

OREGON ★ ★ ★ ★ ★
YOU CAN MAKE A DIFFERENCE

Contacting Lawmakers

To learn about Oregon's legislators, you can go to this website:

www.oregonlegislature.gov

There, you will find information about legislative districts and current legislation.

To contact national and local lawmakers in your area, go to:

www.usa.gov

From the home page, select Government Agencies and Elected Officials.

On the next page, select who you want, such as a senator or mayor.

Type in your home address and click "submit." You will be given the contact information for your local, state, and US legislators.

Voters Speak

Since 1902, Oregonians have had the right to suggest a new law in an initiative and to repeal a law in a **referendum**. First, voters called chief petitioners submit a referendum to the Secretary of State, who must give permission to show the written bill to voters. If enough voters sign the referendum petition, people can make comments for fifteen days. Then the referendum is voted on in the next election.

Former governor John Kitzhaber signs a bill that ended religious discrimination.

In 1923, the Ku Klux Klan convinced Oregon lawmakers to ban teachers from wearing religious clothing in school. The law was directed at Catholic nuns and priests who wore robes and Jewish men who wore yarmulkes (small caps). In 2009, a Muslim student at Portland State University was shocked to learn that teachers had to remove head scarves (Muslim faith), turbans (Sikh faith), and yarmulkes to work in Oregon schools. Teachers and faith-based groups drafted a referendum to repeal that ban. In 2010, voters passed the referendum repealing the law. Signing the law, then-governor John Kitzhaber said, "Repeal is consistent with Oregon tradition that honors individual beliefs, values diversity, and promotes tolerance."

The Willamette Valley has become
known for its valuable vineyards.

Making a Living

Oregon's economy has come a long way from the days when fur trapping and trading were the best ways to earn a living. Oregonians no longer trade for pelts, but other occupations that provided early settlers with a good life continue to do so. Many Oregonians still make a living from the state's rich natural resources—thick forests, fertile soils, and abundant seafood. Of course, many people now pursue a wide variety of new and different occupations.

Forest Products

Since the nineteenth century, Oregon's forests have provided lumber for the entire nation. New houses all over the United States are often built with Oregon lumber. The state is the largest producer of plywood and softwood lumber (such as pine) in the country. Oregon's timber industry is growing as it comes away from the recession in the 2000s, when very few houses were built. In 2013, the logging, wood-processing, paper-making, and other timber-related businesses contributed $12 billion to Oregon's economy. In 2014, one in twenty jobs were forest-related jobs. Oregon's foresters are also developing "**sustainable** forests," by using new tactics to make forests healthy—whether after a forest fire, a logging activity, or an infestation of pests (such as the pine beetle, which has destroyed forests in Montana and Colorado).

Oregon is the largest producer of lumber in the country.

Oregon also leads the nation in the production of Christmas trees, which are grown specifically to be cut down in the winter for the holidays. Oregonians are not the only people who enjoy these trees. Oregon's Christmas trees are shipped throughout the country. In 1991 and in 1992, an Oregon tree was the official White House Christmas tree.

Agriculture

Agriculture is big business in Oregon. In 2014, there were more than thirty-eight thousand farms in the state covering more than 16 million acres (53 million hectares). Unlike many other farming states, 98 percent of farms in Oregon are owned by families, not big corporations. Most of Oregon's farms are located in Marion, Clackamas, Morrow, Umatilla, and Washington Counties. One in eight jobs in Oregon is in farming or ranching.

Oregon is one of the country's most diverse agricultural states. Its climate and soils produce more than 220 different products. Oregon is the number one grower in the country of hazelnuts, blueberries, raspberries, black raspberries, blackberries, boysenberries, and peppermint. Wheat, alfalfa, and hay are other important crops. Oregon farmers also grow grass seeds and landscape plants that are sold throughout the country. Potatoes are a major Oregon crop. Many frozen French fries served in restaurants across the country are made from Oregon potatoes. Although nearly 80 percent of Oregon's agricultural products are sold outside the state, a new trend in farming is called "small farms." These are small local farms that grow vegetables and fruits for sale to nearby restaurants and markets.

Raising cattle is the main agricultural activity in southeast Oregon and it makes the most money of all statewide agricultural businesses. Mostly in western Oregon, the state's dairy farmers care for more than 120,000 dairy cows, which produce two billion pounds of milk a year. Cheese making is another important agricultural industry. The Tillamook County Creamery Association was established more than one hundred years ago and is owned by Tillamook County dairy farmers. It is rated as one of the top ten cheese producers in the world.

Oregon's agriculture industry totaled a record $5.2 billion in sales in 2012. Oregon farmers are some of the most efficient farmers in the world. This means that they achieve high crop yields per acre of land planted.

Historic Locks

The Willamette Locks, opened in 1873, lifted ships and barges forty feet from the lower half of the Willamette River to the upper half, above the falls, until 2011. They are the oldest multi-chambered navigational locks in the United States.

Blackberries grow in abundance in Oregon.

10 KEY INDUSTRIES

Agriculture

Fishing

1. Agriculture

Oregon is a top producer of berries, pears, plums, and cherries. Apples are also grown in the state. Hay is Oregon's second-ranked crop, providing 7 percent of the state's total agricultural income. Grapes for making wine and hops for making beer are increasing in sales.

2. Fishing

Commercial fishers, crabbers, and shrimpers catch albacore tuna, Dungeness crab, bottomfish (such as rockfish), pink shrimp, and whiting. The area is known for its pink, silver, coho, and Chinook salmon fisheries.

3. Food Processing

Food processing is a major manufacturing business. The most important products are frozen fruits and vegetables. Other processed foods include baked goods, beverages, and canned goods. Oregon is particularly known for its frozen French fries, Kettle's potato chips, and Oregon Chai Tea.

4. Livestock

Beef cattle and dairy cows are Oregon's most valuable livestock products. Other livestock businesses are goats, sheep, chicken, and eggs.

5. Manufacturing and Technology

The leading manufactured products are electronic components including oscilloscopes, computer video display monitors, calculators, printer components, microprocessors and communication microchips. Many technology and biotechnology companies are located in Oregon.

6. Nursery Products

Grass seed and greenhouse and nursery products comprise Oregon's number one agricultural sector. Gardeners, homeowners, and landscapers throughout the country buy Oregon grass seed, landscape trees, and daffodil, iris, lily, peony, and tulip bulbs.

7. Real Estate

The third most important service industry is based on real estate. It includes banks, insurance companies, realtors, and developers. There is an increasing amount of development in Oregon, especially resorts and retirement villages.

8. Timber

Building products are the second most important manufacturing industry in Oregon (after technology manufacturing). Oregon is the leading US manufacturer of plywood, veneer, and particleboard.

9. Tourism

Oregon's mountains, forests, waterfalls, beaches, and lakes, which include recreational areas such as such as Mount Bachelor's ski resort and Crater Lake National Park, attract visitors year round.

10. Wholesale and Retail Trade

The second largest service industry (after personal services, such as health care and legal services) is wholesale trade, including foreign automobile imports, and wheat and forest product exports. Sportswear is a large trade industry.

Timber

Tourism

Recipe for Cheddar Cheese Crackers

Cheese crackers are a favorite snack. It's easy to make your own.

What You Need

Rolling pin

Fork

Large bowl

Cookie sheet

Cookie cutter or table knife

Measuring spoons

Measuring cup

½ stick (59.1 milliliters) of butter

½ cup (118.3 mL) of flour (plus extra to use on the counter)

4–5 teaspoons (24.6 mL) of milk

¾ cup (177.4 mL) grated cheddar cheese

¼ teaspoon (1.2 mL) salt

1 tablespoon (14.8 mL) of oil

What to Do

- Get an adult to preheat the oven to 375°F (190°C).
- Oil the cookie sheet.
- Cut the butter into small pieces, set aside.
- Mix the flour and salt in bowl, and add the cheese. Stir with a fork.
- Add the butter and stir with a fork (or hands) until the mixture is crumbly.
- Slowly add cold milk and mix with a fork (or put flour on your hands and mix). Only add enough milk to form a big ball.
- Spread the flour on a counter. Place the ball on the floured counter; flatten it with your hand.
- Roll the dough until it forms a large, thin sheet.
- With a cookie cutter or a knife, cut the dough into small shapes.
- Place the shapes on a cookie sheet and bake for 12 to 15 minutes.
- When the crackers are slightly browned and crispy, remove them from the oven (have an adult help). Let them cool 15 minutes.
- Crunch away!

Fish and Wildlife

Another major industry in Oregon is based on the abundant wildlife in the state. In 2013, Oregon's commercial fishing industry made about $148 million. Commercial fishers hauled in about 2.4 million pounds of salmon and 17 million pounds of Dungeness crab. Shrimp boats brought in nearly $25 million worth of pink shrimp, and other catches included tuna, halibut, and whiting.

The success of salmon comes in no small part because of a joint effort between Native American and non-native commercial fishers, as well as government, scientists, and the citizens of Oregon. The number of salmon returning to Oregon's rivers was declining rapidly in the last decades of the twentieth century because of hydropower dams, water pollution, and over-fishing. Oregonians took action. The government placed limits on fish catches. Environmentalists and communities cleaned up polluted waterways, and new methods to help fish get past the dams were designed and built. In the fall of 2014, nearly 1.6 million Chinook salmon and 1 million coho salmon made their way from the sea to their spawning grounds, breaking a record in place since 1938.

Other businesses related to fisheries include canneries, fish and tackle supply stores, food processors, and restaurants. Oregon has more than 62,000 miles (100,000 km) of fishing streams, more than 1,700 lakes, and, of course, the long Pacific shoreline. The fish in both inland and coastal waters not only provide food for Oregonians and people all over the world—they also provide fun for people who like to fish as a sport. Almost 700,000 people buy fishing licenses each year in Oregon. Salmon and trout are the most popular fish to catch.

People also come to Oregon to hunt. In all, almost 300,000 people—both residents and visitors—buy hunting licenses each year in the state. The animals that are hunted include deer, elk, pronghorn antelope, bighorn sheep, cougars and bears. Waterfowl such as ducks and geese are also hunted.

Minerals are processed into cement at the plant in Weatherby.

Minerals and Metals

Oregon's supplies of natural gas and various minerals have created new and growing industries. For example, one mining company in Grants Pass mines what is known as Oregon blue clay. The clay is used in medicines as an antibacterial that kills germs such as *E. coli*, staph, and salmonella. The Mist Gas Field in Columbia County is the only producer of natural gas in the Pacific Northwest. The first natural gas fueling station for cars that run on natural gas opened in Eugene in June 2014.

Other ways Oregonians make a living include the sale of sand and gravel, cement and lime, crushed rock, and clay. Oregon is a leading producer of pumice stone. Pumice is rock formed by volcanic explosions. It is used in cosmetics, in making concrete, and as an additive to soil. Oregon also has a supply of gold and gemstones, such as agates, obsidians, and sunstones. Aluminum and steel are made in Oregon.

Manufacturing and Technology

Oregon's manufacturing industry is one of the fastest growing in the nation. In 2012, Oregon manufacturing companies made $74 billion, which is nearly 40 percent of the state's economic output. Manufacturing businesses include food processing, building materials, and technology products such as computer hardware, microchips, printers, and other computer-based products. Hewlett-Packard, a company that makes computers and printers, began to do some of its manufacturing in Oregon in the 1970s. The company has a large facility in Corvallis. A division of Symantec—which makes computer programs and provides other computer-related services—has offices in Eugene. Intel, an international technology company, has seven centers in Oregon and is now the largest private employer in the state. Genentech, a giant biotechnology company that makes many important cancer drugs, is located in Hillsboro.

There are numerous new start-up technology companies in the Portland area. Like the nickname "Silicon Valley" (silicon being a material used in making computers) was given to the area where Apple and Google and countless other California technology companies are located, the Portland area also has a nickname for its cluster of high-tech companies: "Silicon Forest."

Services and Tourism

The service industry takes in more money than any other industry in Oregon. This industry includes businesses such as insurance companies, wholesale trade, retail stores, hospitals and health-care companies, law firms, real estate businesses, banks, schools, and colleges. Transportation is also considered part of the service industry, along with television and radio stations and telephone and cable companies.

Businesses providing services for tourists are part of the service industry as well. Oregon's tourism industry took in more than $9 billion in 2013. Tourism is very important to Oregon's economy and all regions of the state bring in tourism dollars. On the coast there are sea caves, marine mammals, aquariums, art galleries, historic sites, lighthouses, and an amusement park. Riverside communities benefit from tourists who come to raft, kayak, fish, or windsurf. Communities in the central and eastern portions of the state see tourists enjoying outdoor recreational activities, as well as galleries, shops, museums, and theater. When tourists come to the state, they not only spend money on hotels, restaurants, museums, casinos, and natural and historic sites—they also provide jobs, because someone has to serve them. Waiters at restaurants benefit from tourists, as do tour guides and people who own gas stations, ski resorts, rental shops, and other businesses.

Oregon is considered one of the most beautiful states in the nation, with its sandy beaches on the Pacific Coast, its tall, snow-capped mountains in the interior, and its high deserts in the east. The natural beauty draws Oregonians outside, rain or shine, and makes them feel proud to be living in a place where the trees grow tall, the rivers run clear, and people greet one another with enthusiastic smiles.

★OREGON★
STATE MAP

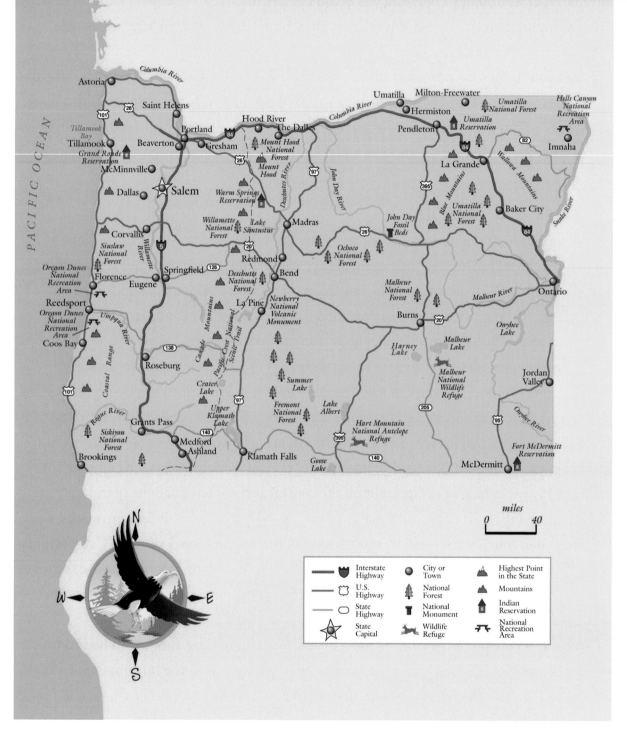

Columbia River

Astoria

Saint Helens

101 26

Tillamook Bay

Tillamook

Beaverton

Portland

Gresham

Hood River

The Dalles

Columbia River

Umatilla

Milton-Freewater

Hermiston

Umatilla National Forest

Hells Canyon National Recreation Area

Pendleton

Umatilla Reservation

82

PACIFIC OCEAN

Grand Ronde Reservation

McMinnville

Dallas

Salem

Mount Hood National Forest

Mount Hood

Warm Springs Reservation

Deschutes River

John Day River

97

La Grande

Wallowa Mountains

Imnaha

395

Blue Mountains

Baker City

Willamette National Forest

Lake Simtustus

Madras

26

John Day Fossil Beds

Umatilla National Forest

84

Corvallis

Siuslaw National Forest

Willamette River

5

Springfield

126

Redmond

20

Bend

Ochoco National Forest

Snake River

Oregon Dunes National Recreation Area

Florence

Eugene

Cascade Mountains

Deschutes National Forest

La Pine

Newberry National Volcanic Monument

Malheur National Forest

Malheur River

Ontario

Reedsport

Oregon Dunes National Recreation Area

Coos Bay

Umpqua River

138

Pacific Crest National Scenic Trail

Burns

20

Harney Lake

Malheur Lake

Onyhee Lake

Coastal Range

Roseburg

Crater Lake

Summer Lake

Malheur National Wildlife Refuge

Jordan Valley

101

Rogue River

Siskiyou National Forest

Grants Pass

Upper Klamath Lake

97

Fremont National Forest

Lake Albert

205

Onyhee River

95

Brookings

Medford

Ashland

140

Klamath Falls

Goose Lake

Hart Mountain National Antelope Refuge

395

Fort McDermitt Reservation

140

McDermitt

miles

0   40

N
W   E
S

Interstate Highway	City or Town
U.S. Highway	National Forest
State Highway	National Monument
State Capital	Wildlife Refuge

Highest Point in the State	
Mountains	
Indian Reservation	
National Recreation Area	

OREGON
MAP SKILLS

1. What is the northwestern-most city in Oregon?

2. Does the Deschutes River flow east or west of the Cascade Mountains?

3. If you were in Portland, which direction would you go if you wanted to go to Jordan Valley?

4. What river flows through Grants Pass?

5. What city lies between the Blue Mountains and the Wallowa Mountains?

6. What is the southern-most coastal city in Oregon?

7. What river flows by the town of Hood River?

8. Name the two US highways that go over the Cascade Mountains.

9. How many major lakes can you find in southern Oregon?

10. Is the Warm Springs Reservation east or west of the Cascade Mountains?

Boatnik Parade in Grants Pass

Rogue River

10. East
9. Seven
8. US Highways 20 and 26
7. Columbia River
6. Brookings
5. La Grande
4. Rogue River
3. Southeast
2. East
1. Astoria

State Flag, Seal, and Song

Oregon is the only state whose flag has a different design on the front and on the back. The flag is navy blue with gold lettering and designs. Blue and gold are the state colors. On the front of the flag (shown below) are the state seal and the year Oregon was admitted as a state: 1859. On the reverse side is a golden image of a beaver, referring to Oregon's nickname, the Beaver State.

The state seal was adopted in 1857. In the seal itself, a bald eagle sits on top of a shield, which shows the sun setting over the Pacific Ocean. Mountains and forests represent the natural resources of Oregon. A covered wagon stands for the pioneers who came to Oregon. A plow, a sheaf of wheat, and a pickax stand for the state's early agricultural and mining industries. Two ships represent the victory of the United States over Britain in controlling the land that became Oregon. Around the shield are thirty-three stars (Oregon was the thirty-third state).

"Oregon, My Oregon," with words by John Andrew Buchanan and music by Henry B. Murtagh, won a contest in 1920 and was adopted as the state song in 1927. The lyrics can be found on this website: www.50states.com/songs/oregon.htm.

Glossary

conservation   The careful use of natural resources to prevent them from being lost or wasted.

estuary   A body of water formed where the ocean meets the lower end of a river.

extinct   When a plant or an animal is no longer living.

fossil   A preserved remnant of a plant or animal from an older geologic age.

glaciers   Slow-moving masses of ice and rock.

gorge   A narrow, steep, walled canyon.

Great Depression   The worldwide economic collapse after the stock market crashed in 1929. High unemployment lasted through much of the 1930s.

initiative   In government, a procedure where citizens can propose a law and vote to have it approved.

lava   Hot, melted rock that issues from a volcano or crack in the earth.

missionaries   People who travel to places far from home to spread religious beliefs and/or to help people who are poor or sick.

nomads   People who move from place to place, taking their belongings with them.

obsidian   A dark natural glass formed by the cooling of hot lava.

referendum   In government, a procedure with which citizens can propose to repeal a law and vote to have the repeal approved.

reservation   An area of land in the United States that is kept separate as a place for Native Americans to live.

sustainable   Using methods that do not completely use up or destroy natural resources.

More About Oregon

BOOKS

Harasymiw, Mark. *The Bizarre Life Cycle of a Salmon*. New York : Gareth Stevens, 2013.

Harness, Cheryl. *The Tragic Tale of Narcissa Whitman and a Faithful History of the Oregon Trail*. Washington, DC: National Geographic Society, 2006.

Robinson, Kate. *Lewis and Clark Exploring the American West*. Berkeley Heights, NJ: Enslow Publishers, 2010.

Sanford, William R. Nez Percé *Chief Joseph*. Berkeley Heights, NJ: Enslow Publishers, 2013.

WEBSITES

The Official Oregon State Website
www.oregon.gov

Oregon Blue Book Kids' Page
bluebook.state.or.us/kids

The Oregon Historical Society
www.ohs.org

Visit Oregon
www.traveloregon.com

ABOUT THE AUTHORS

Ruth Bjorklund lives on an island in Washington State. She has written more than forty books for young people. Her family loves heading to Oregon to spend time in the outdoors.

Joyce Hart fell in love with writing while she was a student at the University of Oregon. She raised her children in Eugene and is currently a freelance writer.

Jacqueline Laks Gorman has been a writer and editor for more than thirty years. The New York native and her family live in DeKalb, Illinois.

Index

Page numbers in **boldface** are illustrations. Entries in **boldface** are glossary terms.

African Americans, 43, 50–51

agriculture, 66–67
   See also farming

animals, 5, 9, 18–20, **19**, 23–24, 40, 71

Asian Americans, 47, 50

birds, 19

capital, *See* Salem

cities, *See* Corvallis; Eugene; Portland; Salem

Clark, William, *See* Lewis and Clark

climate, 4, 7, 13, 17, 66

coast, 6, **6**, 9, 13, 16–17, 23, 25–26, 28, 71, 73

conservation, 42

Corvallis, 9, 35, 52, 73

economy, 39–40, 47, 65, 73

education, 51–52

estuary, **28**

Eugene, 9, 34, 52, 54, 72–73

extinct, 19

factories, 39–40

farming, 31, 40, 46–47, 50–51, 66–67

fossil, 13–14

glaciers, 12, 15

gorge, 12, **13**, 14, 16, 53

government, 26, 33, 39, 46, 48, 57–59, 61, 63

governor, 40, 43, 53, 57–59, 61–63

Great Depression, 39

Hispanic Americans, 51

initiative, 61, 63

Jefferson, Thomas, 28

lava, 8, 14–15, 28

laws, 19, 40, 50–51, 57–59, 61

Lewis and Clark, **22**, 29, **29**, 31–32

Lewis, Meriwether, 28

manufacturing, 40, 68–69, 72–73

missionaries, 31–33, 36, 45–46

mountains, 7–8, 17, 26, 42, 69, 73
   Bachelor, 12, 35, 54, 69
   Blue, 12, 16, 20, 32, 75
   Cascade, 9, 12, 32, 52, 75
   Hood, **8**, 12, 15, **15**, **44**
   Rocky, 28–29, 33
   Wallowa, 12, 15–16, 26, 75

native, 5, 19, 23, 25, 29

Native Americans, 14, 21, 23–29, **24**, **26**, 31, 36–37, **36**, 45–47, **47**, 51, 57, 71

nomads, 23, 43, 45

obsidian, 25, 28, 72

Pacific Ocean, 7–9, 17, 28–29, 76

Pendleton, 12–13, 16, 31–32, 55

Portland, 9, 16, 32, 34, **34**, 38–40, 47, **50**, 52–53, 55, 59, 73, 75

Index

railroads, 35, 37–39, **38**, 45–47

referendum, 63

reservation, 26–27, 37, 42, 52, 75

rivers, 7–9, 23, 25–26, 42, 71

    Columbia, 5, 7, 16, 19, 24, 26–29, 31, 34, 39–40, 43, 47

    Deschutes, 5, 16, 24, 35, 53, 75

    Rogue, 15–16, 24, 35, 37, 53

    Snake, 5, 7, 12, 16, 31

    Willamette, **9**, 10, 31, 34, 40, 53, 67

Sacajawea, **22**, 29

Salem, 9, 31, 34, **34**, 39, 55, 58

settlers, 17, 25–26, 29, 33, 36–38, 40, 46, 50, 57, 65

slavery, 50–51

sustainable, 65

technology, 34–35, 68–69, 72–73

universities and colleges, Oregon State University, 5, 35, 52

    Portland State University, 52

    Reed College, 52

    University of Oregon, 34, 52, **53**

    Willamette University, 52